PLAY THERAPY ACTIVITIES
FOR MINDFULNESS

Play Therapy Activities for MINDFULNESS

80 Play-Based Exercises
to Improve Emotional Regulation and Strengthen the Parent-Child Connection

Melissa LaVigne, LCSWR, RPT-S

ROCKRIDGE
PRESS

First Rockridge Press trade paperback edition 2022

Rockridge Press and the Rockridge Press logo are trademarks or registered trademarks of Callisto Media Inc. and/or its affiliates in the United States and other countries and may not be used without written permission.

For general information on our other products and services, please contact our Customer Care Department within the United States at (866) 744-2665, or outside the United States at (510) 253-0500.

Paperback ISBN: 978-1-68539-096-9
eBook ISBN: 978-1-68539-782-1

Manufactured in the United States of America

Interior and Cover Designer: Mando Daniel
Art Producer: Megan Baggott
Editor: Annie Choi
Production Editor: Jael Fogle
Production Manager: Jose Olivera

All illustrations used under license from Shutterstock.com, except for the following: © M. by mprintly/ Creative Market, cover background. Author photo courtesy of Karen Monaco.

10 9 8 7 6 5 4 3 2 1 0

This book is dedicated to my husband and children, who keep me playing and growing every day.

Contents

— CHAPTER 5 —
Sensory Awareness 45

— CHAPTER 6 —
Imaginative Stories & Metaphors 63

— CHAPTER 7 —
Grounding Games 81

— CHAPTER 8 —

Mindful Art & Music 97

— CHAPTER 9 —

Connecting with Nature 115

Introduction

Welcome to *Play Therapy Activities for Mindfulness*! My name is Melissa LaVigne, and I am a play therapist and a parent. I have been working with children clinically for ten years in schools, community mental health settings, and private practice.

Being a parent or caregiver can be one of the most rewarding experiences in life, and it can also be one of the most challenging. Children spark joy, love, and feelings of connection, but not without some heartache and difficult moments. As a therapist and parent, I find that one of the most powerful tools for navigating parenting challenges is connecting to myself, my children, and the world around me.

So how can we connect with ourselves and develop a greater connection with our children? One simple and powerful way to do this is by learning to speak the universal language of children: play! Play is how children connect with themselves, others, and the world. It is through play that children solve problems, build friendships, and process their experiences. Children's relationship with play is what inspired me to make play and play-based interventions a cornerstone of my work.

Some years ago, I started to experience burnout. Perhaps it was trying to do it all or not quite knowing how to meet my own needs first before helping others—a sentiment that many therapists, parents, and caregivers often share. I started to lose passion in my daily work and, most important, I was struggling to hold compassion for myself.

It was during this time that I found yoga and started to study mindfulness. I quickly experienced the benefits these practices offer and noticed their playful nature. I started to feel reconnected with myself and my work. Practicing mindfulness taught me how to cultivate compassion within myself first and, in turn, cultivate it in others. I saw that I could apply mindfulness to my play-based work to promote deeper connections and healing. From these experiences, I realized that mindfulness-based play can help children thrive, heal, and grow. Today, I am constantly looking for ways to integrate mindfulness into my work as a therapist.

Mindfulness can seem difficult to practice, like a mystical state only certain people can achieve. Such thinking is based on a misunderstanding of what mindfulness is. Mindfulness at its core is simple. Dr. Amy Saltzman, a holistic physician and mindfulness coach, describes it beautifully: "Mindfulness is learning how to pay attention on purpose with kindness and curiosity." Practicing mindfulness has been proven to increase our ability to nurture self-compassion, hold focus, manage emotions, and connect with ourselves and others. Most children are naturally capable of this type of playful and attentive curiosity, whereas we adults often need reminders on how to be mindful.

This book is filled with eighty play-based activities that will help you and your child practice mindfulness while having fun together. You can use the activities in this book to help children learn more about their feelings, improve focus, and practice impulse control, as well as to strengthen the bond that you already share. Strong bonds between caregivers and children can increase a child's self-esteem, emotional regulation, and so much more. I applaud your willingness to start on this important journey. Now let's enjoy some mindful playtime together!

CHAPTER 1

Play Therapy for Kids

P lay therapy is a powerful tool that can generate change, growth, and healing in children. Before we dive into the play-based activities in this book, it is important that we explore some of the concepts behind play therapy. In this chapter, you will learn about the roots of play therapy and the basic framework that many play therapists follow when working with children in a therapeutic setting. You will also learn the differences between play therapy and the kinds of play children engage in naturally. (Note that although you can play with your child in ways that are beneficial, such play should not be a replacement for formal treatment, if warranted.)

What Is Play Therapy?

Fred Rogers, host of the preschool television series *Mister Rogers' Neighborhood*, is famously quoted as saying, "Play is often talked about as if it were a relief from serious learning. But for children play is serious learning. *Play is really the work of childhood*" (emphasis added). Rogers was keenly aware of a fundamental truth: Play is the way children grow, develop, and learn. Although children play to relax and experience joy, play can also be a powerful tool.

According to the Association for Play Therapy, play therapy is defined as "the systematic use of a theoretical model to establish an interpersonal process wherein trained play therapists use the therapeutic powers of play to help clients prevent or resolve psychosocial difficulties and achieve optimal growth and development." Put more simply, play therapists use a variety of play-based tools and strategies to expand and enhance the therapeutic process and make it more accessible for children.

As early as the 1920s, psychologists recognized that children use play to manage their emotions, improve their skills, and develop insight into their experiences. But it would take another twenty years or so before these concepts were established as a formal therapeutic method. As play and play-based approaches were formalized and studied, researchers discovered that play therapy isn't powerful just because it is a more kid-friendly way of doing therapy; they found that the very essence of play is healing. Play aids in the development of attachment, the bond a child has with their caregiver. It can improve self-expression as well as the management and regulation of emotions and stress. Play also strengthens a child's resilience, thereby improving their ability to manage challenges throughout their lifetime.

Most therapists who work with young children ages three to nine use some form of play therapy. Many schools, hospitals, doctor's offices, and mental health clinics have moved to training and hiring therapists who have experience with play therapy techniques.

How Play Therapy Works

One of the most vital aspects of therapy for anyone, at any age, is the need to feel safe. Engaging children through play is necessary to build a feeling of safety and connection in a therapeutic setting. Once a child feels safe with the therapist, they can begin the many stages of healing and growth that occur throughout the therapeutic process.

Almost all therapies, play therapy included, follow a framework for treatment. This framework starts by creating a sense of safety and rapport between the therapist and family. Next, most therapists develop a treatment plan or goals they are working toward with the family and child. This might include emotion identification, impulse control, anxiety management, coping strategies, and trauma processing.

Every play therapy session is different, because each one is geared toward meeting the needs of the child in that moment. Some sessions might involve loud, messy, and energetic play, while others might include gentle, focused, and slow play. To an untrained observer, a play therapy session might not look much different from "just play." Throughout the session, the therapist is focused and attentive, gently guiding the play to help the child achieve the goals of treatment. Many times, this might include the therapist engaging in role-playing, storytelling, using toy figures in a sand tray, or even playing what appears to be a silly, nonsensical game. All of these interactions have intention and purpose in the therapeutic process.

Play therapy uses many different theories and practices. Two of the most well-known frameworks are nondirective and directive, described in the next sections. Many play therapists integrate skills and tools from both styles.

Nondirective Play Therapy

Nondirective play therapy allows the child to use their natural language of play to direct the treatment session. A nondirective play therapist sets the stage for treatment by allowing the child to play in the therapy space in any way they like. In this way, the child can work through issues at their own pace.

Directive Play Therapy

Directive play therapy uses specific play-based interventions that are led and directed by the therapist. This approach is different from nondirective, where the child leads the session. Directive play therapy often takes commonly used therapeutic techniques, such as teaching coping skills, and makes them more developmentally appropriate for a child by using play.

Key Play Therapy Techniques

This section describes common strategies and techniques used by play therapists. The intention of this section is not to teach you how to be a play therapist, but rather to give you a better understanding of what play therapy might entail.

Toys and Objects

Play therapists will have toys and objects readily available. Often toys will be available on easy-to-reach open shelves. This allows the child to choose the toys they need and want to use.

Metaphors and Storytelling

Metaphors and storytelling are used to describe a situation similar to the one the child may be experiencing without actually talking about the child. This approach allows the child to feel safe and more distant from their own challenges until they are ready to work directly with their issues. Many children use metaphors and storytelling naturally, and the therapist will gently guide or work with the metaphor the child has already created.

Role-Play

Role-play is often used as a way for a child to gain mastery or feel powerful in a challenging situation. A great example of this is preparing for a medical appointment. Having the child play the role of doctor and the therapist play the role of child allows the child to feel in control, which can help them feel more prepared and capable when the appointment actually occurs.

Creative Arts

Creating art—like painting, drawing, making music, crafting, and so on—is a powerful tool of expression that many play therapists use.

Imagery and Fantasy

Imagery and fantasy help children use their imagination to overcome challenges. For example, the therapist might encourage the child to imagine that their daily anxiety is a small worry monster that lives in their mind, and they can beat this monster by becoming a courageous knight.

Game Play

Children can learn impulse control, turn taking, emotional regulation, and many other social skills through games. Games are often used to learn and practice new skills in developmentally appropriate ways.

The Benefits of Play Therapy

Psychologist and neuroscientist Jaak Panksepp found that play develops the areas of the brain needed for emotional regulation, impulse control, creativity, and more. These early developments create impacts on the brain that last throughout the course of one's life. In the early 2000s, researchers at Harvard Medical School found that having a level of playfulness throughout one's life could impact a person physically and emotionally long into retirement. This study also found that creativity, which is derived from playfulness at a young age, is directly connected to an individual's feelings of happiness and health.

Play has also been found to greatly improve an individual's executive functioning skills. These are the skills used for problem-solving, planning, awareness of time, and much more. In addition to the impacts that play has on the brain, play also strengthens the bond between a child and their trusted caregivers. Research in interpersonal neurobiology, the study of how the body and mind are impacted and shaped through our relationships, has found that frequent playful and joyous connections between a child and their caregiver can strengthen that child's ability to regulate their emotions, manage impulses, and develop resilience throughout their life.

Because play can create a level of safety and connection that talking alone does not, through play a child can take charge of a painful topic, create alternative scenarios, and experience power over a situation that perhaps they felt powerless in. The safety of the relationship and the metaphorical distance play creates enable a child to visit and process big, uncomfortable feelings.

Here are some of the concrete benefits a child can gain from play therapy:

- Increased feelings of safety and connection with others
- Ability to fully experience and express emotions
- Greater understanding of and ability to use coping strategies
- Greater creative problem-solving skills
- Capacity to interpret physical and emotional needs
- Ability to manage challenging emotions such as anger, sadness, worry, shame, and anxiety
- Capacity to process grief and loss
- Ability to create positive and healthy relationships
- Ability to overcome the impacts of trauma
- Increased resilience
- Improved sense of self and self-esteem

CHAPTER 2

Mindfulness Meets Play Therapy

This chapter highlights the many benefits of mindfulness and how you can create powerful change in simple ways. Bringing mindfulness into parenting can help shift the way you see yourself as a caretaker. Also, growing your understanding of mindfulness will allow you to engage your child in mindfulness-focused play.

What Is Mindfulness?

Have you ever stopped to take in a deep, full breath and tried to appreciate the moment you're in? Have you ever noticed your thoughts coming and going without getting lost in them? If you answered yes to either of these questions, you may have practiced mindfulness!

Dr. Amy Saltzman describes mindfulness as paying attention on purpose, with kindness and curiosity. When we practice mindfulness, we try to stay in the moment, noticing our thoughts, sensations, and experiences as they occur. Developing mindfulness is part of many different cultures and spiritual traditions. Although meditation is the most well-known way to practice mindfulness, it is not the only way. In fact, we can bring mindfulness into our everyday lives in simple, playful ways.

Research has shown that teaching children to explore the world in a mindful way has many benefits. It can improve focus, emotional regulation, self-concept, impulse control, and much more. As these benefits become more well-known, teachers, therapists, and caregivers are using mindfulness with children in many different areas. Many schools are even starting to use these practices with children as young as three to teach emotional awareness and coping skills.

The Seven Pillars of Mindfulness

Jon Kabat-Zinn, a scientist and leader in the mindfulness field, has identified seven pillars of mindfulness. These seven pillars are derived from his work in the creation of mindfulness-based stress reduction (MBSR). The MBSR program is an evidence-based practice of mindfulness that reduces stress and promotes healing, and has been in use since the late 1970s. MBSR is now practiced all over the world and has been found to support individuals in cultivating inner resources and coping skills and reducing stress. The seven pillars work together, each one supporting the other to build a strong mindfulness practice.

Nonjudging

Nonjudgment is paying attention to what is happening without getting lost in our opinions, thoughts, and judgments. The brain's tendency to judge is a built-in survival mechanism. We are constantly evaluating each moment as good, bad, or neutral. Practicing nonjudgment encourages us to simply notice the here and now.

Patience

Patience is vital when cultivating mindfulness. We cannot force ourselves or anyone else to be more mindful, in the same way you cannot force your child to eat or use the bathroom. We must have patience with ourselves as we develop this skill.

Beginner's Mind

This pillar is one that children already practice and often experience. Beginner's mind is allowing yourself to experience a moment with fresh eyes, as if you have never experienced it before, like the way children do when they try something for the first time.

Trust

Trust is another pillar that children often hold naturally, but a lifetime of experiences makes this harder for adults to achieve. This pillar involves the simple act of trusting your gut and believing in your own authority, instincts, and wisdom.

Nonstriving

Nonstriving is a bit of a paradox because it is so simple yet can feel so challenging. Nonstriving is the art of nondoing—just inviting and noticing what is happening in the moment without any expectation or goal to create a different experience from the one you are currently having.

Acceptance

Accepting things as they are doesn't necessarily mean passive resignation. Rather, it is a willingness to see things for what they are in the moment. The more we can keep our mind in the present moment, the more we can see how quickly things change. When we combine awareness of how quickly circumstances can shift with our ability to accept each changing moment, we find peace in the present moment.

The more we practice mindfulness, the more we might notice our difficulty in letting things go. It is human nature to catalog each moment and hold on to it. The effort of letting go is key to being present in the moment. When we don't attach too much to a moment, we can accept it for what it truly is.

The Benefits of Mindfulness

Mindfulness can benefit anyone at any age, from young children to adults. What is especially useful about mindfulness is that you can apply the skills in a variety of situations. For example, I was teaching an after-school mindfulness class to a group of elementary students. One day, I received a message from the classroom teacher about how this group of students had applied mindfulness. A student had become extremely upset, and right in the middle of his emotional outburst, two other students spontaneously approached him and reminded him of his powerful breath. They worked as a group to help the upset child find his breath and return to a calm state. These children had mastered the ability to generalize the mindfulness skills outside of the after-school setting and use them in the present moment! Mindfulness gave them practical tools to help a struggling friend manage his emotions.

Here are some other benefits of practicing mindfulness:

- Reduces negative self-talk
- Increases compassion for oneself
- Reduces the negative impact of stress
- Decreases the impact and frequency of rumination and/or obsessive thoughts
- Decreases anxiety and depression
- Improves ability to identify one's emotions
- Improves ability to handle, regulate, and express emotions
- Increases present-moment awareness
- Improves quality of sleep
- Increases compassion for others

Now that you understand what play therapy is as well as the benefits of mindfulness, let's explore how the two can complement each other.

Using Mindfulness in Play and Play Therapy

Play with a mindfulness focus involves engaging in playful activities that are designed to teach both adults and children how to stay in the present moment. For parents and caregivers, mindfulness practices can help them notice their own emotional responses and reactions during difficult situations, allowing for better connections with their children.

In therapeutic settings, play therapists use mindfulness-based practices to teach the child specific skills in a play-based way while incorporating the seven pillars of mindfulness. Through play therapy with a mindfulness focus, a child can overcome many of life's challenges by improving their understanding and expression of emotions, strengthening and building a positive self-concept (their view of themselves), increasing impulse control, and developing self-calming skills. A mindful play therapist along with directive mindfulness activities can create a powerful path for healing and growth.

It is important to highlight the distinction between play therapy with a mindfulness focus and the play-based activities you will find in this book. These activities are intended to help you engage with your child in a playful way through the lens of mindfulness. Although some of the activities are similar to ones a play therapist might engage a child in during a play therapy session, they have been adapted to be appropriate for the scope of play between a parent/caregiver and child in a home setting.

The Benefits of Play Therapy with a Mindfulness Focus

When a child is angry, sad, or not listening, it can trigger challenging emotions for a parent. In these difficult moments, parents can often have flashbacks to their own childhood experiences, even reliving the shame and anger they felt as a child. When this happens, they can lose their ability to be present with their child and provide them with a sense of safety through their calm and grounding presence. Parents and caregivers can use mindfulness strategies to create

From Playing to Prospering: A Play Therapy Success Story

The combination of play therapy and mindfulness can create powerful change. My client Julie (confidential information has been changed for privacy) came to play therapy at the age of eight because she was struggling with her parents' divorce. Her mom noticed that Julie became extremely overwhelmed by her emotions and didn't know how to express them, often getting physically aggressive with her mother and siblings.

Julie started by engaging in weekly play therapy sessions. Over the course of treatment, Julie worked on expressing her emotions and processing the impact of her parents' divorce. In addition to benefiting from the healing powers of child-centered play therapy, Julie learned coping skills through playing games with a mindfulness focus. She practiced noticing her feelings as they came and choosing safe, healthy ways to express her emotions. Julie's mom noticed that her daughter was starting to use the tools she learned in therapy, like naming what she was feeling in the moment, staying present with the emotion, and then practicing healthy ways to express that emotion. Over time, Julie no longer needed weekly sessions and was feeling confident in her ability to notice her feelings and handle them in a healthy way!

insight and present-moment awareness. The more aware we are of our own emotional reactions and triggers based on our life experiences, the more attuned and present we can be to our child's needs.

Not only does play with a mindfulness focus create the opportunity to connect to the present moment, our own experiences, and our child's experiences, it also creates a developmentally appropriate way for children to learn this skill, especially because mindfulness is not easily taught verbally. When a child can engage with the tool of mindfulness in a play-based way, they are more likely to be able to generalize the use of this tool in their daily life. In addition, when a parent is present and aware of their own emotional reactions, they are more likely to be able to help their child find calm in the moment. When you as the parent are calm during your child's distress, you automatically create an avenue for soothing that they can follow. The more that you and your child engage in play with a mindfulness focus, the more likely you will be able to find grounding and calm even in difficult moments.

Positive Outcomes for You and Your Child

Play therapy with a mindfulness focus can produce positive changes in children and adults when used regularly and consistently. Some of the potential benefits of mindfulness for parents/caregivers and children include:

Parent/Caregiver–Child Connection: Helps develop a strong connection, the first step in creating any behavior change in your child.

Emotional Expression & Regulation: Allows both you and your child to identify and express your emotions. An increased ability to regulate, or control, your own emotions and reactions allows you to be the calming force your child needs when they are experiencing big emotions.

Grounding & Coping Skills: Similar to coping skills, grounding skills work to bring you into the present moment, not just find calm. Regulated doesn't always mean calm, but rather our ability to manage our emotional reactions in the moment. Grounding skills help us stay in the present moment enough to use a coping strategy.

Mind–Body Connection: Helps you and your child develop greater awareness of how the mind and body interact in the present moment.

Stress & Anxiety Management: Improves the ability to tolerate and manage anxiety and stressful experiences.

Present-Moment Awareness: Being focused on our current experience, right in this moment. During present-moment awareness, we are not thinking about the past or the future, only attending to what we notice right now.

Focus & Attention: Focus is our ability to attend to one activity, interest, or task at a time. Attention centers around our ability to take notice of someone or something.

Self-Compassion & Confidence: Helps increase self-compassion, which is vital in cultivating self-love, positive self-image, and resilience in challenging experiences.

Creativity & Flexible Thinking: Creativity is the ability to use our imagination and develop original ideas. Flexible thinking is being able to think about something in a new way. It can assist in adjusting to unexpected changes or problem-solving a change.

Executive Functioning Skills: Improves ability to manage time, order information, and follow directions.

Impulse Control: Gives children fun opportunities to practice managing impulsive behaviors and reducing conflicts.

Calm & Relaxation: Improves your child's ability to fall asleep and stay asleep, leading to more restful nights and joyful days.

CHAPTER 3

Tools & Tips for Mindful Play

In this chapter, you will learn how to get the most out of this book. You will discover helpful tools and tips for building positive playtime using mindfulness. Although you may not be new to playing with your child, the following will help you feel even more confident as you dive into the activities.

Listen and Let Your Child Lead

Sometimes as parents and caregivers we can forget how little control children have. Most of our child's day is determined by someone else. But children need to experience a sense of power, mastery, and control. These moments create a sense of safety and are important developmentally. Many times, when children are acting out or displaying challenging behaviors, it is because they feel unseen and like they have no control.

Play with a mindfulness focus is a great way to create an experience where your child can have control and feel powerful. When you engage your child in this type of play, the intention is to foster connection and create a sense of equal or shared power. As the parent or caregiver, you are working to exemplify the pillars of mindfulness (discussed in chapter 2) to help cultivate this type of connection. Your child will benefit not only from the opportunity to feel in charge in the moment, but also the experience of really being seen by you.

To create this type of presence and connection, try simply delighting in your child by letting them lead and be the center of the moment. Avoid the temptation to multitask, for instance, by cleaning up or answering emails during play. Try to just *be* with your child during these moments. What does this look like? It can be playing on the floor with your child at their eye level or following their lead without judgment or expectations. If at some point you feel like trying to change or shift the play into something other than what your child is creating, pause. Take a deep breath and remember the value in your child having the experience of being in charge. Try to verbally track what they are doing in that moment, as if you are a sports announcer. This might sound something like "Oh, you know just what to do with that! Now you're putting it on the table. Awesome move!" Being with your child in this way amplifies their experience of being seen and grows their connection to you.

Creating a Safe and Playful Space

Play with a mindfulness focus can take place just about anywhere with few to no supplies. That's because this type of play is rooted in the relationship you already have with your child. No matter the size of your play space, or lack thereof, it will be just right! What will make the play space perfect is the energy and intention you bring to the activities as you engage in them with your child. Less is more when it comes to engaging your child in play with a mindfulness focus. Your play space doesn't need fancy toys or objects. Simple household items, common toys, and basic arts and crafts materials will be the only extras needed outside of your relationship with your child.

As the parent/caregiver, you already hold the power and ability to make your child feel physically and emotionally safe, seen, and valued during each activity. The more you are present and connected with your child, the safer they will feel.

In addition to presence and connection, there are some other simple strategies you can use to keep the play experience safe and enjoyable. One strategy is to set limits during play. As you play with your child and follow their lead, it is still important to keep them safe and within the limits of your home. If you are not comfortable with your child jumping on the couch or running in the house, for example, you can still set that boundary. A simple yet effective way to do this would be to say something like "I see you want me to chase you through the house. In the house, we use our walking feet. I can chase you on my walking feet or even on my silly creeping toes instead." This sets a limit while giving the child a choice and still engaging in play.

Another strategy could be used with a child who struggles with transitioning out of an activity. Getting special playtime with a parent or caretaker is exciting for a child and can be hard to give up. If your child is likely to become upset or have a tantrum when playtime is over, consider using a visual timer for the activity. Have your child set the timer prior to the start of playtime; this allows them to have a sense of control and a visual awareness of how long the time will last. Remember that you are still the parent/caregiver. Following your child's lead does not mean tossing all the rules out the window!

How to Make the Most of This Book

The activities in this book have been created with children ages three to nine in mind. As the parent or caregiver, you are the expert on your child. Therefore, as you go through the activities, use your judgment to choose those that feel best suited for your child, regardless of their age. All the activities in this book work individually, so feel free to jump around from chapter to chapter to find the activity that works best for you and your child in the moment.

The eighty activities and games are divided among six chapters. Initial activities explore the body, breath, and movement. The last chapter offers mindfulness activities that can be enjoyed outdoors. Each activity page outlines the duration of the activity, potential benefits, materials needed (if any), and step-by-step instructions. Many of the activities offer tips for modification or off-the-page suggestions to make playtime even more mindful.

One of my favorite activities is called "Notice Mind" (page 98). This activity teaches a silly song that helps your child get ready to leave the house. Almost every parent I have ever met would agree that getting a child dressed, ready, and out the door can be extremely stressful. Notice Mind is a simple yet playful way to prompt mindfulness, possibly shifting a stressful moment into a positive one.

Activity Quick Reference

Use this chart to help you locate activities that strengthen specific skills. Each activity is categorized, identifying the areas it can help with.

Potential Benefits	Activities
Parent/Caregiver– Child Connection	• Together Breaths (page 28) • Stuffy Talks (page 75) • Mindful Hockey (page 89) • Back Art (page 92) • Notice Mind (page 98)

Potential Benefits	Activities
Emotional Expression & Regulation	• Butterfly Hug (page 31) • Power Pose (page 36) • Jumping Feelings Scale (page 48) • Feelings Song (page 57) • Weather Report (page 65) • The Feelings Wave (page 71)
Grounding & Coping Skills	• Mirror Breath (page 35) • Breathing Times (page 40) • Sunshine and Snow Clouds (page 93) • Barefoot Breathing (page 121)
Mind–Body Connection	• Iceberg Rescue (page 53) • Body Check (page 86) • Human GPS (page 95) • Music Mind (page 106) • Mindfulness Hike (page 123)
Stress & Anxiety Management	• Lumberjacks (page 33) • I Am a Tree (page 69) • My Favorite Color (page 72) • Magic Carpet Ride (page 77) • Feel My Feelings (page 105) • Worry Bug (page 112)
Present-Moment Awareness	• Taste Experiment (page 50) • Puppy Mind (page 64) • Word Focus (page 85) • Mud Pie Magic (page 120) • Mindful Walking Path (page 124)
Focus & Attention	• Ring-a-Ding-Ding (page 58) • Music Hide-and-Seek (page 59) • Focused Tree (page 82) • Artistic Focus (page 99) • Freeze Wand (page 118)

CONTINUED»

Potential Benefits	Activities
Self-Compassion & Confidence	• Hugging the World (page 39) • Animal Sidekick (page 74) • Mantra Stone (page 102) • I Am Unique (page 104) • Kindness Bands (page 110)
Creativity & Flexible Thinking	• Artist Eyes (page 60) • Movie Magic (page 70) • Imagine a World (page 73) • Pass the Story (page 94) • Scribble Thoughts (page 100) • Trash Mind (page 111)
Executive Functioning Skills	• Mountain Wiggle (page 34) • Space Explorer (page 47) • Movie Magic (page 70) • Morning Hunt (page 87) • Camera Eyes (page 91)
Impulse Control	• Slow-Motion Moves (page 29) • Personal Space Bubble (page 32) • Mindfulness Jar (page 55) • Focused Tree (page 82) • Wiggle, Jump, Freeze, Walk (page 83)
Calm & Relaxation	• Body Scan, Body Layers (pages 30 and 46) • Push It (page 54) • Ceiling Watch (page 76) • Sound Vibrations (page 109) • Breathing in Color (page 117)

CHAPTER 4

Body, Breath, & Movement

One of the easiest ways to learn mindfulness is by connecting to our bodies, breath, and movement. In this chapter, you will find fun movement activities that teach your child how to notice their body in the moment. You'll move your bodies in a mindful way to build self-confidence and emotional regulation. You will help your child learn different ways to find power in their breath. Our breath is one of our most powerful tools, and it can shift or even completely change our response to any situation in the moment. The final activities in this chapter provide playful ways for you and your child to create a greater connection using movements that require concentration. The more we are aware of our bodies, the more regulated, grounded, and compassionate toward ourselves we can become.

Together Breaths

When children are upset, angry, or in the middle of a tantrum, offering your calming presence can sometimes be enough to help them find calm. This simple yet effective breathing activity encourages you and your child to practice breathing in sync. Practice this skill in moments of calm so you can use it when big feelings start to arise.

BENEFITS: Emotional Expression & Regulation, Parent/Caregiver–Child Connection, Grounding & Coping Skills

1. Start in a comfortable seated position, with you and your child facing each other. Make sure you are close enough that your knees are touching.

2. Next, place your hand over your child's heart and have your child place their hand over your heart.

3. Together, take a deep breath, breathing in very slowly through the nose for a count of three, then breathing out through the mouth for a count of five.

4. Notice how the breath is moving in and out of each other's bodies. See if you and your child can sync your breathing rhythm.

5. Try to feel each other's heartbeat changing speed with each breath.

6. Complete as many breaths as feels good in the moment.

KEEP PLAYING: Feel free to modify how you are sitting. Some children might prefer sitting back-to-back or would rather sit in your lap, snuggled up as you breathe together, trying to match each other's rhythm.

Slow-Motion Moves

This activity can help your child explore and notice sensations in their body. Life moves quickly, and we do not slow down often enough to really notice how our bodies feel. Playing this silly slow-motion game with your child is a fun way to help them start noticing the connection between their body and the present moment.

BENEFITS: Mind–Body Connection, Present-Moment Awareness, Self-Compassion & Confidence, Impulse Control

MATERIALS: Any type of music

1. Start by explaining to your child that you will both try to move your bodies at different speeds, and try to notice how your bodies are feeling *right now*.

2. Decide with your child what type of body movements you want to do, like dance, shake, wiggle, jump, or practice ninja moves. Get creative!

3. Choose music that you and your child can both enjoy moving to. As you move, try to notice how your body is feeling. Say out loud what you notice, and ask your child to do the same. For example, *Are your legs burning or feeling tingly? Is your forehead sweaty?*

4. Next, choose a slow song that you can move your body to in slow motion. Try to do moves similar to the ones you did before. Notice how different it feels to move in this slow way. Say out loud what you notice, and ask your child to do the same.

MASTER MINDFULNESS TIP: Ask your child to try to connect their breath to each movement. The more they can connect their breath with their movements, the more awareness they can develop.

Body Scan

In this activity, you will help your child notice one part of their body at a time. As they go through each part of their body, they might start to notice sensations they feel in the moment. The more your child is able to connect with their body, the easier it will become for them to identify and express what they need.

BENEFITS: Mind–Body Connection, Emotional Expression & Regulation, Calm & Relaxation

1. Find a comfortable place in your home for your child to lie down.

2. Ask your child to close their eyes or look down toward the floor. Tell them to notice their breath as they breathe in and out. Suggest they notice their belly moving up and down with each breath. Pause to allow your child time to notice their breathing.

3. Now tell them to notice their feet. See if they can feel all the way down into their feet and toes. See if they can feel their whole foot. Pause briefly.

4. Next, move to their legs. See if they can feel their ankles, knees, and whole leg. *Are they feeling cold or hot? Tired or full of energy?* Pause briefly.

5. Next, move to the belly. Ask your child if they can notice their belly moving up and down with each breath. Pause briefly.

6. Now move to the arms and shoulders. *Are they feeling tight and hard like uncooked spaghetti or loose and wiggly like cooked spaghetti?* Now see if they can notice their fingers. *Are they hot or cold? Do they feel shaky or still?* Pause again.

7. Have your child start to notice their mouth, nose, eyes, and the top of their head. Finally, have them notice their whole body, from their toes to the top of their head. Tell them to take a deep breath in and out while they slowly wiggle their fingers and toes. Finally, tell them to slowly open their eyes.

8. After your child has completed the body scan, talk about what was easy and what was hard about noticing different parts of their body.

MASTER MINDFULNESS TIP: This is a great activity to do right before bed. Scanning the body can help your child get calm and feel grounded.

Butterfly Hug

It is best to teach and practice calming breaths and movements when your child is calm. They can benefit from these tools in the middle of a tantrum or big feeling—but that is not the time for them to be learning them! Exploring mindful calming tools will build up their skills and help both of you use them during difficult moments. The butterfly hug works to calm the body through both the breath and nervous system. It was first used by Lucina Artigas in the early '90s to support survivors of Hurricane Pauline in Acapulco, Mexico.

BENEFITS: Emotional Expression & Regulation, Grounding & Coping Skills, Calm & Relaxation, Stress & Anxiety Management

1. Have your child cross their arms over their chest, resting their hands just below their shoulders. If it feels comfortable, they can interlock their thumbs, creating the shape of a butterfly.

2. Next, tell them to take a deep full breath, in through their nose and out through their mouth.

3. As they breathe in deeply and slowly, have them begin to gently tap their hands on their chest by lifting their hands and then placing them back down, as if their hands were butterfly wings.

4. Have your child do this for as long as it feels good, as they continue to work to notice their breath.

KEEP PLAYING: Grow the connection between you and your child by telling them things you love about them as they give themselves a butterfly hug. Mention a recent moment when you were proud of them or a simple thing they did that made you smile. When you delight in your child, you strengthen your bond, which in turn will improve your child's behavior and self-love.

Personal Space Bubble

The goal of this activity is to help your child learn their body boundaries. Building a connection with our bodies and understanding what makes us feel safe and unsafe is a powerful tool! Throughout this activity, you will explore together how it feels to be the boss of your body and how much personal space feels comfortable.

BENEFITS: Impulse Control, Mind–Body Connection, Self-Compassion & Confidence

1. Explain to your child that they will be playing a game where they get to decide how much personal space they need to help their body feel safe.

2. Next, decide who will be the body boss and who will be the body invader.

3. From across the room, the invader walks toward the body boss slowly and quietly.

4. The body boss raises a hand as a stop signal when they feel the invader is getting too close. Once the invader sees the body boss raise their hand, the invader must freeze where they are.

5. Now switch roles, with the invader becoming the body boss and the body boss becoming the invader.

MASTER MINDFULNESS TIP: This is a great way to teach your child about body autonomy, a concept that will support your child throughout their life. You can even talk about other people in your child's life who might be allowed to get closer or kept farther away from their personal space.

Lumberjacks

Sometimes we feel sluggish. Maybe we had a long day at work or our child woke up with low energy. This activity is a great way to get energized when you're both feeling less than 100 percent. Noticing how sensations change through this simple, playful movement is a great way to practice being present.

BENEFITS: Emotional Expression & Regulation, Mind–Body Connection, Stress & Anxiety Management

1. Give your child the following instructions:

   a. *Pretend you are in a forest, and there are tall trees all around you. You just cut down a large tree and now you are going to chop it into smaller pieces of wood.*

   b. *You are so strong to have cut down that big tree! Stand tall and strong. (Have your child set their feet slightly wider than hip distance apart.)*

   c. *Imagine you are holding an ax. Lock your fingers or wrap one hand around the wrist of your other hand. Take in a full breath and bring your hands up over your head.*

   d. *Imagine you are swinging your ax down hard to chop the wood!*

   e. *Breathe out as you let your arms drop toward the ground. Bend forward and let your hands swing between your legs.*

2. If you wish, do the actions along with your child.

3. Repeat as many times as you like!

MASTER MINDFULNESS TIP: Have your child try to match their breath with their movements and notice how their body feels. Ask them if their body feels different or the same.

Mountain Wiggle

This activity focuses on building concentration through physical body connection. You and your child will be working to wiggle one part of your bodies at a time. Although it sounds simple, it takes focus and control to wiggle and be silly with only part of the body!

BENEFITS: Impulse Control, Mind–Body Connection, Focus & Attention, Executive Functioning Skills

1. Have your child stand with their arms at their sides. Remind your child to keep their body safe, even though you are both about to be silly.

2. Start wiggling your bodies. Ask your child to notice just their feet. Have them wiggle just the toes, then rock back and forth on the feet.

3. Ask your child to notice their legs. Have them wiggle their legs slowly at first, then super fast. Move to different areas of the body. Have your child notice and wiggle their hips, hands, arms, shoulders, and head.

4. Finally, have your child wiggle their whole body all at once. Let them wiggle for ten to fifteen seconds. Wiggle along with your child! You can help your child transition back to a still body by counting down, saying, *We will wiggle until I get to one. Find a still body in three, find a still body in two, find a still body in one!*

5. Once you both become a still standing body, take a deep breath in together.

MASTER MINDFULNESS TIP: Play this game in reverse for an added challenge. Start by wiggling the whole body, then stop wiggling one body part at a time, until your bodies are totally still. This order takes a lot more concentration and focus.

Mirror Breath

Mirror breath is a simple and playful way to learn deep breathing, which research has found to be the most soothing type of breathing we can do. For deep breathing, we exhale longer than we inhale. This signals our body that it is safe and can rest, which is the key to calming down.

BENEFITS: Stress & Anxiety Management, Focus & Attention, Grounding & Coping Skills, Emotional Expression & Regulation

MATERIALS: A mirror, window, or other reflective surface

1. Find a mirror or window in your home that your child can get close enough to that they can almost kiss the surface.

2. Tell your child to inhale through their nose for a count of three.

3. Have your child exhale with their mouth open toward the mirror or window. Tell them to breathe out long and hard so they can fog up the glass! Encourage them to breathe out for at least a count of four (or more, if possible).

4. Repeat a few times, letting your child fog up the mirror as much as possible.

KEEP PLAYING: Prompt your child to add a little art to the foggy surface with messages like *I love you*, a positive affirmation like *I am strong*, or emotion faces.

Power Pose

Our nervous system plays a powerful role in regulating our emotions. When we experience a challenging or traumatic event, our nervous system stores information from the event. This is how our body has evolved over time to keep us safe. The problem is that the information stored in our body can cause us to respond negatively or out of proportion to a situation that we perceive as similar to the previous challenging or traumatic experience, even when it is not the same. This activity can help our bodies regulate and manage our emotions in the present moment without overreacting.

BENEFITS: Emotional Expression & Regulation, Mind–Body Connection, Self-Compassion & Confidence

1. Ask your child to think of an upcoming experience or event that they want to go well, like their first dance recital or riding a bike.

2. Together, identify how your child wants to feel during the experience or event— for example, brave, calm, powerful.

3. Ask your child to show you with their body what it might look like when they feel that way. This might look like standing with hands on hips or arms reaching up toward the sky—any way they pose their body is okay! This position will be their *POWER POSE*.

4. Next, ask them to think about the opposite feeling and pose. For example, the body might be curled into a tiny ball, or the shoulders might be slumped, with head down. This pose will be their *STUCK BODY*.

5. Now have your child start in their *stuck body* pose and notice how it feels to be in this pose. When they feel ready, have them quickly move into their power pose!

6. As they hold their power pose, have your child imagine they are doing the thing they want to accomplish. Ask them to say how they want to feel using a powerful "I" statement; for example, *I am brave!* or *I can do it!*

7. Repeat this activity as many times as your child wishes. Be sure they say their power statement out loud at the end.

MASTER MINDFULNESS TIP: Amplify this activity by copying what your child is doing and saying. Do the same motions as they move from stuck body to power pose. Repeat their power statement, encouraging them to say it in a strong, loud voice. For added fun, have your child stand on their bed as they say it. When your child feels big and tall, it can intensify the positive experience in their body.

Mindful Jungle Exploration

In this activity, you will engage in active mindfulness by creating an imaginary jungle in your home. Active mindfulness is intentionally paying attention to how our body feels as we move and breathe. Have fun exploring mindfulness with playful movement, imagination, and a focus on the breath!

BENEFITS: Focus & Attention, Present-Moment Awareness, Mind–Body Connection

MATERIALS: Pillows, stuffed animals, blankets, chairs, laundry baskets

1. Use the suggested materials or anything you have on hand to create an imaginary jungle path in your home.

2. Next, take your child through these steps:

   a. *Take a deep breath in.*

   b. *Notice each part of your body and give it a little wiggle. Start with your feet. Now wiggle your legs, belly, hands, arms, shoulders, and head.*

   c. *Let your attention spread to your whole body. Now you are ready to explore!*

3. Ask your child to move slowly and silently through the jungle path in their mindful body. Guide them with questions such as *How do your feet feel? What is it like when you move your legs and arms?*

4. Remind them that if their mind starts to wander, they should bring it back to their mindful body by focusing on their feet.

5. Have your child walk the jungle path a few times, each time trying to stay present in their mindful body.

KEEP PLAYING: Make this as silly as you want. Your child can pretend to be different jungle animals, crawling, slithering, jumping, or running along the path. The sillier the movement, the harder it becomes to notice just one part of the body.

Hugging the World

The goal of this activity is to help your child practice offering love and kindness to others. Loving-kindness is a cornerstone of mindfulness practice. Research shows that the more we practice loving-kindness, the happier we become.

BENEFITS: Self-Compassion & Confidence, Grounding & Coping Skills

MATERIALS: Paper and coloring materials (optional)

1. Have your child imagine the whole world or draw it on a piece of paper. Talk about the places your child has been, like the park, their school, or even somewhere far away your family may have traveled to.

2. Ask your child to think about places in the world they haven't been to but would like to visit—maybe Disney World, Africa, or the North Pole!

3. Have your child imagine sending loving, kind thoughts to everyone and everything in the world by using the following script:

   a. *Imagine that you are giving the whole world a big hug. This hug is so big, it includes places you go every day, like school, and places you have never been.*

   b. *Take a big breath in. Lift and spread your arms open wide, wide enough to fit the whole world in.*

   c. *Now exhale, and send your sweetest, kindest, most loving thoughts to the whole world!*

4. Repeat the activity several times.

KEEP PLAYING: Once your child has completed this activity, have them continue to draw pictures of the world filled with their love and kindness. Ask them to imagine what the world might look like if it was filled with only love and kindness.

Breathing Times

Our breath is one of our most powerful mindfulness tools. Finding playful ways to engage in mindful breathing with children will increase their ability to use their breath as a resource in challenging times. In this activity, you will use a timer to see how many or how few breaths you and your child can complete in just one minute!

BENEFITS: Grounding & Coping Skills, Calm & Relaxation, Emotional Expression & Regulation

MATERIALS: Timer of any kind

1. Start by deciding if you want to practice slow breathing (inhaling for three and exhaling for five) or even breathing (inhaling for four and exhaling for four).

2. Next, determine a length of time that feels right for you and your child. This could be one minute, two minutes, or thirty seconds.

3. Start the timer and try to notice how many or how few breaths you and your child can accomplish! Keep track by putting a finger up each time you inhale.

4. Remind your child to breathe in through the nose and breathe out through the mouth.

MASTER MINDFULNESS TIP: Have your child try to focus only on the sensations of their breath, not the time on the clock. How does the air feel as it enters their nostrils, and does it feel different as it leaves their mouth? Ask them to notice how their lungs feel when they are filled with air. The more sensations your child notices, the more they are in the moment.

Heart and Body Dance

Learning to connect with our bodies can be challenging for both children and adults. We can strengthen this connection by creating exaggerated physical experiences in the body. A fun and simple way to do this with your child is by putting on some music and dancing away.

BENEFITS: Mind–Body Connection, Emotional Expression & Regulation

MATERIALS: Music

1. With your child, choose the music that you want to move to.

2. Help your child quickly scan their body before you begin. You can say something like *Let's try to notice how our body feels before we start.* Ask them to pay attention to their heartbeat and notice if it is beating fast or slow.

3. Turn on the music and start dancing. The goal is to move energetically enough to change your heartbeat.

4. After a couple of minutes, pause the music and stop dancing.

5. Ask your child to stand still and take in a deep, full breath with you, breathing in through the nose and out through the mouth.

6. Have your child quickly scan their body, as in step 2. Bring their attention to their heartbeat. Ask them if their heart is beating faster or slower.

7. Dance for a few more minutes and have your child check their heartbeat again. Ask them if it seems the same as before or different.

KEEP PLAYING: Pick a slow, quiet song and try moving your bodies more slowly, swaying or wiggling in slow motion. After a few minutes, pause the music and have your child check their heartbeat. Ask them how dancing to slow music has changed their heartbeat.

Animal Moves

This activity uses simple, common yoga poses as a playful way to experience mindful movement. When we do new or challenging movements, we send the message to our bodies that we are strong. When our body feels this way, it can build up our self-confidence.

BENEFITS: Self-Compassion & Confidence, Mind–Body Connection, Parent/Caregiver–Child Connection

MATERIALS: Yoga or exercise mat (optional)

1. Sing the following (to the tune of "The Farmer in the Dell") as you and your child move your bodies:

   Reach my hands up high, (stand with feet shoulder width apart, arms reaching toward the sky)

   Dive them down low, (fold forward at the hips with arms hanging loose)

   Bring them back to the sky, Mountain Pose. (return to standing with hands overhead)

2. Add a challenge with more movement and song:

   Walk my feet back nice and slow, this is Plank Pose. (do a plank pose resting knees on the ground if needed)

   Belly to the ground, it's time to be a snake, sssssss, it's fun to be a snake. (lie your stomach and place hands under the shoulders, gently lifting head and neck)

   Hips to the sky, it's time to be a dog, woof, woof, woof, it's fun to be a dog. (press down into your hands as you lift the hips toward the sky, keeping feet on the ground)

   Jump to my hands, it's time to be a frog, ribbit, ribbit, ribbit, it's fun to be a frog. (step forward so your feet meet your hands)

   Arms to the sky, raise them up high, standing like a mountain, strong and tall. (return to standing with hands overhead)

KEEP PLAYING: After you have mastered the song and movements, try to do the whole sequence at different speeds. Try doing it really fast or really slow.

CHAPTER 5

Sensory Awareness

Creating a connection between our mind and body, in a mindful way, has many benefits. Our feelings and experiences are energetically stored in our bodies. Many times, our bodies might respond to a situation in a particular way before our mind even realizes we are reacting to it. Despite this strong link, many of us ignore the mind–body connection. From a young age, children are often taught to ignore the feelings in their bodies. The more this happens, the less able they are to interpret their body sensations as information and important clues for determining what they need. Mindfulness helps your child relearn and foster this vital life skill! The activities in this chapter offer playful ways for your child to further explore this by building a mindful connection between their five senses: hearing, touching, tasting, smelling, and seeing.

Body Layers

This activity is a simple way for your child to increase their awareness of physical sensations. By visualizing different layers of their body, children learn to be present in their physical self, in the moment. This activity is a great way to practice settling the mind through focused attention.

BENEFITS: Mind–Body Connection, Focus & Attention, Calm & Relaxation

1. Find a comfortable place for your child to sit or lie down. This could be their bed, a couch, or even the floor.

2. Guide your child through taking a few deep, full breaths. Your child can choose to close their eyes or look down at the floor.

3. Once your child is ready, direct them through the layers of their body by reading the following script in a slow, calm voice:

   a. *Try to notice a sensation or feeling that is happening on the outside layer of your body. Maybe it's something you notice happening on your skin. (pause briefly)*

   b. *Now try to notice a sensation or feeling somewhere just inside your body, maybe right under your skin. (pause briefly)*

   c. *Now see if you can notice a sensation or feeling deeper inside your body, maybe in your tummy, head, or heart. (pause briefly)*

   d. *On your next breath in, open your eyes.*

4. Have your child share the sensations and feelings they noticed in the different layers of their body.

MASTER MINDFULNESS TIP: For younger children, ask them to share out loud what they noticed after each layer before moving on to the next. This is a great game to play before bed or for a task that needs lots of focus, like homework.

Space Explorer

In the seven pillars of mindfulness, beginner's mind is the practice of seeing everything with fresh eyes. This activity is a great way to help your child foster this ability through intently noticing their surroundings.

BENEFITS: Focus & Attention, Executive Functioning Skills

1. Choose a place or room in your home that your child will pretend is a new planet they have discovered.

2. Prompt your child to enter this space as if they have never been there before.

3. As your child explores this new "planet," ask them if they notice something that is different or has changed, or maybe something they never noticed before.

4. Have your child continue to explore and notice changes on this planet or move to other planets (rooms) in your house.

KEEP PLAYING: If your child struggles to notice things, create obvious changes in the space before the activity begins. Take turns, with your child making changes to the "planet" and then asking you to figure out what has changed.

Jumping Feelings Scale

Identifying our emotions is the first step in understanding how to be present with our feelings. The more we are aware of our feelings, the more we are able to know how to respond in a healthy way. This activity uses a visual scale to represent feelings intensity to help build emotional awareness and acceptance in a playful way.

BENEFITS: Emotional Expression & Regulation, Grounding & Coping Skills, Stress & Anxiety Management

MATERIALS: Writing materials, 10 pieces of paper, stuffed animals or books (optional)

1. Start by creating a scale from 1 to 10. You can write each number on a separate piece of paper and line them across the floor, or line up 10 toys or books to represent the scale.

2. Explain to your child, using the following script, that the scale represents how big feelings can get:

   a. *Sometimes feelings seem small, like they're just a one. We can handle them and they're not taking over. Maybe there was a time you felt annoyed, but you could keep doing what you were doing and didn't need help with your annoyed feeling.*

   b. *Sometimes feelings seem big, like a ten. We might need help managing a feeling like that. We need to totally stop what we're doing and just "be" with the feeling!*

   c. *Sometimes feelings are somewhere in the middle, like a five. They're not tiny, but not huge either. We can "be" with the feeling, get a little support, and continue on.*

3. Next, create a list of lots of different emotions. Your list might have *happy, sad, worried, nervous, embarrassed, scared, excited,* and *annoyed,* to name a few.

4. Work with your child to recall different moments when you both have felt each of those feelings. For each emotional experience, identify how big the feeling felt on the number scale.

5. Encourage your child to move their body along the scale by jumping, skipping, running, or walking slowly. Only offer movement choices that feel safe and appropriate for your space.

6. As you identify different feelings together, avoid trying to fix your child's responses or reactions. The goal is for them to notice their feelings and how big they are. This builds emotional acceptance and tolerance.

MASTER MINDFULNESS TIP: As the parent or caregiver, it is okay for you to share honest and age-appropriate feelings with your child. For example, you might say, *I felt angry today when my order came and was missing things. My anger felt like a five.* The more we model emotional awareness and acceptance, the more accessible these skills become for our children.

Taste Experiment

Mindful eating teaches us how to be present with the food that is in our mouth, engaging our senses of taste, smell, and touch. Often we rush through our meals or are glued to a screen as we eat. It can be strange and challenging to slow down the process, making it an intentional practice. This mindful eating activity modifies a classic mindfulness practice to make it more developmentally appropriate for children.

BENEFITS: Focus & Attention, Present-Moment Awareness

MATERIALS: Snack food

1. Select a food you are comfortable with your child eating outside of mealtime. It should be small enough for them to hold in their mouth for a few moments, like Goldfish crackers, raisins, or M&M's.

2. Explain to your child that they are going to do a fun experiment. Have them find a comfortable seat and close their eyes.

3. Read the following script in a calm, gentle voice:

    a. *Take a deep breath, in through your nose and out your mouth. Notice how your body is feeling. Does your tummy feel hungry? Is your mouth dry? (pause briefly)*

    b. *Now open up your hand. I am placing a small snack in your hand. Notice how it feels. Is it rough? Is it soft? Is it smooth or bumpy? (pause briefly)*

    c. *Now I am going to hold the food right under your nose. Try to notice how the snack smells. Does it smell salty or sweet? As you smell it, is it making your stomach grumble or your mouth water? (pause briefly)*

    d. *Open your mouth and stick out your tongue. I am going to place the snack in your mouth. Don't start chewing right away! Just let it sit on your tongue. How does it feel on your tongue? How does it taste—salty or sweet? Is it smooth or bumpy? (pause briefly)*

e. *Start to chew your snack. Notice how it changes. Use your whole mouth to explore it. When you are ready, tell me what you noticed and what snack you ate!*

4. Switch roles if you like, allowing your child to place a snack on your tongue as you try to guess what it is.

MASTER MINDFULNESS TIP: Modify this activity to fit your child. Some children might want to keep their eyes open or talk about what they are noticing out loud. You are the expert on your child, so follow their lead.

Name That Sound

The goal of this activity is to help your child connect to their sense of hearing. Practicing noticing different sounds is a great way to connect to the present moment. The more we are in the here and now, the more mindful we become.

BENEFITS: Focus & Attention, Executive Functioning Skills

MATERIALS: Household items, nature sounds

1. Gather different items in your home that can produce a variety of sounds, such as a pot or a box of pasta. You can also select different nature sounds on YouTube or your phone.

2. Have your child close their eyes.

3. Make or play different sounds. After each sound, ask your child to guess what the sound was.

4. Take turns with this activity, with you closing your eyes as your child produces different sounds for you.

5. Repeat as many times as you like, using as many objects or sounds as you and your child can think of.

MASTER MINDFULNESS TIP: Take this game outdoors on a nice day! Sit in a park or in your yard and try to notice the different sounds around you. Take guesses about where each sound came from.

Iceberg Rescue

This activity heightens your child's sense of touch through a very intense sensation—by touching something very cold!—and allows your child to connect with their senses in the present moment. Note that this activity takes a bit of pre-activity preparation.

BENEFITS: Focus & Attention, Emotional Expression & Regulation, Mind–Body Connection

MATERIALS: Ice cube tray; small plastic toys; plastic bin or bowl of any size; spray bottle, pitcher, or measuring cup

1. To prepare for this activity, collect a handful of your child's small plastic toys that are small enough to fit in an Ice cube tray (for example, Legos, counting bears, bugs, mini cars).

2. Fill the ice cube tray with water and place a toy in each section. Set the tray in the freezer until the water is completely frozen.

3. Remove the ice cubes from the tray and place them in the bin. As you do, ask your child questions about the texture and temperature of the ice cubes, saying something like *Do your fingers feel hot or cold when you touch the cubes?*

4. Offer your child a container you feel comfortable with them using to pour water from, such as a small spray bottle, pitcher, or measuring cup.

5. Allow your child to work at rescuing their toys frozen in the ice cubes.

KEEP PLAYING: This is a great activity for you to practice the art of letting your child lead. Let them be in charge of rescuing their toys while you announce each step they take! Stay present and silly by sitting at their eye level.

Push It

When a child is overwhelmed or irritable, they are less likely to be in the here and now. Play that activates the nervous system, specifically through **proprioceptive input**, helps ground the body. Proprioceptive input involves the way our body moves in space or our ability to interpret how we are moving. Children can struggle with this for a variety of reasons. This game of Push It can create the sensation of heavy work in the body, turning on the proprioceptive system and grounding the body in the moment.

BENEFITS: Grounding & Coping Skills, Present-Moment Awareness, Calm & Relaxation

1. Ask your child if they want to use all their strength to try to knock you over or push down the house.

2. If they choose the house, have them pick a wall that they will try to push. Instruct them to plant their feet firmly on the ground and, using all their might, push the wall over!

3. If they choose you, position yourselves to face each other. Depending on the height, age, and physical strength of your child, you might choose to sit or stand. Interlock your hands with your child's. Instruct your child to push into your hands with all their strength.

4. Once they finish pushing, guide them to take two deep breaths, inhaling and exhaling slowly.

MASTER MINDFULNESS TIP: Have your child try to match their breath with their movement. Instruct them to breathe in before they start pushing and exhale for as long as they push.

Mindfulness Jar

Helping children read their body cues so they can meet their needs is a powerful way to help them build awareness of their sensations. A mindfulness jar is a simple way to do this.

BENEFITS: Mind–Body Connection, Impulse Control

MATERIALS: Jar or container of any kind, snack, drinks, fidget toys, trinkets, ice pop sticks, sandwich bags

1. Identify items that you feel comfortable making available to your child at any time. Only choose items that you are sure you can say yes to. These items should work to meet different needs your child might have, including snacks, juice boxes, and cups for water, as well as items for sensory needs (for example, poppets, Play-Doh, paper, or a small bag of Legos).

2. Fill the jar with the items and explain how it works:

   You are learning to be a mindfulness master. One way to do this is by noticing what you need in the moment. Sometimes it might be a drink or something sweet. Another time it might be a special toy, or even something to rip! You can use the things in the jar anytime you need them. When you want them, the answer will always be yes!

MASTER MINDFULNESS TIP: Give the jar a bedtime! It could be after teeth have been brushed. You might say, *The yes jar will always have a bedtime, just like you! Once the yes jar is in bed, we can no longer get things from it.*

Layers of Sound

This activity is a challenging yet powerful way for your child to connect to the sounds around them and bring them into the present moment. You will guide your child to notice sounds originating from varying distances, starting with sounds far away and moving to sounds nearby.

BENEFITS: Present-Moment Awareness, Focus & Attention, Calm & Relaxation

1. Have your child settle on a chair or the floor, or lie on a couch.

2. Ask your child to close their eyes, if they are comfortable doing so.

3. Walk them through the following steps, reading them out loud in a calm voice:

   a. *Take a deep breath in through your nose and let it out through your mouth. Now see if you can stretch your listening all the way to the outside of our house. See if you can notice a sound happening outside. (pause briefly)*

   b. *Now bring your listening to the inside of our house. See if you can notice a sound happening inside. (pause briefly)*

   c. *Now see if you can shrink your listening to really close to you or even to the inside of you. See if you can hear your own breath or your heartbeat. (pause briefly)*

   d. *Now allow your listening to spread out to the whole room. Take a deep breath in and open your eyes.*

4. Have your child discuss the different sounds they heard and what felt easy or hard about this exercise.

MASTER MINDFULNESS TIP: Depending on your child's age and ability to focus, you might ask them to verbally share what they notice after each step.

Feelings Song

A simple way to teach a child how to manage overwhelming emotions is to model different tools when you are becoming overwhelmed yourself. This activity teaches you a silly yet effective way to move through your own overwhelmed emotions and help your child build this skill.

BENEFITS: Grounding & Coping Skills, Emotional Expression & Regulation

1. When you're feeling overwhelmed, sing the following song (to the tune of "London Bridge Is Falling Down"). Modify the song to best describe what you are feeling:

   I am feeling really mad, really mad, really mad. I am feeling really mad right now. I could breathe or take a break, take a break, take a break. I could breathe or take a break right now. (pause to breathe)

2. As you sing this song, feel free to add more steps you could take to help manage the emotion, such as breathing, crying, or taking a break from the situation.

3. You may also modify the song to help your child identify what they are feeling in the moment by listing a few feelings you might be noticing they are feeling:

   Are you feeling mad or sad, mad or sad, mad or sad? Are you feeling mad or sad right now? It's okay to feel that way, feel that way, feel that way. It's okay to feel that way right now.

MASTER MINDFULNESS TIP: Sing this song when you are struggling with keeping your cool. After, say out loud how your body and mood changed after the song.

Ring-a-Ding-Ding

This quick and easy game is a great way to practice paying attention. Using simple items in your home, you and your child will intently tune in to just your ability to hear.

BENEFITS: Impulse Control, Focus & Attention

MATERIALS: Pot and spoon, bell, or chime

1. Choose an object you have around your home that you can use to make a ringing or dinging sound. You could use a pot and spoon, a bell of some kind, or anything else you have on hand.

2. Next, explain to your child that the goal of the game is to keep their body still until the ringing sound stops.

3. Take in a deep breath together.

4. As you and your child exhale, hit the pot or ring the bell. Encourage your child to try to keep their body still until the sound is completely gone.

5. Take turns, with your child ringing the items next. If you are using multiple items, see which items ring longer.

KEEP PLAYING: You can change up this game by choosing a silly dance or movement that you and your child will do until the sound stops. Or you could make it a guessing game by having one person close their eyes and listen to the sound, trying to guess which item made it.

Music Hide-and-Seek

This activity is a fun spin on the classic kids' game hide-and-seek. It helps your child focus on sounds in the moment. When we create opportunities for our child to notice one sensory system at a time, we are helping them build their awareness skills.

BENEFITS: Focus & Attention, Impulse Control, Present-Moment Awareness

MATERIALS: Wireless Bluetooth speaker, cell phone, or music box

1. Choose a device that makes music that you are comfortable with your child holding and hiding throughout your home.

2. Decide which of you will be the hider and which one the seeker.

3. Set the device to start playing music of any kind, at a volume you feel comfortable with.

4. The seeker closes their eyes. The hider takes the device and hides it somewhere in the home.

5. As in the traditional game of hide-and-seek, the seeker stays in place with eyes closed until the hider returns, or alternatively, until the seeker reaches the count of ten.

6. The seeker tries to follow the sound and locate the hidden device.

7. Once the seeker has found the device, switch roles and play again.

MASTER MINDFULNESS TIP: Increase the challenge by lowering the sound coming from the device or by playing sounds that are harder to locate, such as white noise, birds chirping, or recorded household sounds.

Artist Eyes

The goal of this activity is to help your child practice noticing the world with a beginner's mind. Learning one pillar of mindfulness at a time is a great way to practice mindfulness. This game takes concentration and creativity, which is a great combination for learning the skill of beginner's mind.

BENEFITS: Present-Moment Awareness, Focus & Attention, Creativity & Flexible Thinking

MATERIALS: Coloring materials

1. Choose a room in your home or a safe outdoor space for the activity.

2. Have your child walk around and try to notice everything in the space. Instruct them to try to take a picture in their mind of each item.

3. Leave the space and go to another area. Have the coloring materials handy.

4. Ask your child to try to draw as many details of the space they were just in as they can. Their goal is to try to create an accurate picture of the space, without going back to peek.

5. Once the drawing is complete, go back to the space with it and have your child compare it to the space to see how close they were.

MASTER MINDFULNESS TIP: Have your child imagine doing this activity only in their mind. Instruct them to take a mental picture of the space, close their eyes, and try to imagine and describe every detail. Visualization is an advanced and challenging skill for both children and adults, so don't worry if your child needs to grow into this skill.

Animal Dance

This game is a spin on the classic childhood game Simon Says. Anytime we are challenged to pair intent listening with movement, we are building attention and impulse control skills. This game is a fun and silly way to create that challenge for your child.

BENEFITS: Self-Compassion & Confidence, Focus & Attention

1. Explain the rules of the game. One of you will be the animal, and the other will be the caller. The goal is for the caller to try to get the animal to dance at the wrong time.

2. If you are the caller, begin the game by saying *All animals dance!* Your child, the animal, should then dance in response.

3. As your child dances, name a bunch of different animals, objects, foods, and places, for instance, *all chairs dance, all waterfalls dance, all cookies dance,* or *all dogs dance.*

4. The animal can dance only when the caller says the name of any type of animal.

5. If the animal dances at the wrong time, they are out! Switch roles and play the game again.

KEEP PLAYING: Pick specific dance moves to go with different animals. When that animal is named, the person who is the animal has to do that movement. You can make this game as challenging or silly as you want!

CHAPTER 6

Imaginative Stories & Metaphors

Children naturally use their imagination to understand and manage their experiences and the world. The activities in this chapter help children amplify this natural skill while intertwining mindfulness. Some activities use metaphors as a simple and effective way to help the child build an understanding of what mindfulness is. Other activities focus on practicing the mindfulness skill of visualization through guided imagery that you will walk your child through in developmentally appropriate ways. The chapter ends with activities that allow your child to hone what they have learned about mindfulness through dramatic and interactive play. All these activities will help strengthen the bond you share with your child and, in turn, increase their self-confidence and emotional regulation.

Puppy Mind

Mindfulness can be a difficult concept for a child to understand. Using a metaphor and playful activity is a great way to teach them how to come back to the present moment. One of the key aspects of mindfulness is being aware of how our thoughts can be a bit chaotic (like a puppy running all over) and learning how to kindly slow our mind down.

BENEFITS: Present-Moment Awareness, Impulse Control, Executive Functioning Skills

1. Explain the idea of "puppy mind" using the following metaphor:

   Our minds are sometimes just like a puppy. They can move really fast and be all over the place! Mindfulness helps our puppy minds learn how to gently notice one thing at a time.

2. Next, pick who will be the puppy and who will be the mindfulness master.

3. The person playing the puppy will start by being energetic, barking and running around, doing their best puppy impersonation.

4. After a few moments, the mindfulness master will say, *Freeze.*

5. The puppy will freeze, take in a deep breath, and name one thing they see.

MASTER MINDFULNESS TIP: For an added challenge, see if your child can notice what is happening in their mind when they go from silly to still. This will help them start to transfer their mindfulness skills from the metaphor to real life.

Weather Report

This activity uses weather to help children connect to and communicate their emotions. Learning how to understand and express our emotions is challenging. Using a simple metaphor like the weather is a great way to help your child interpret what they are feeling in the moment.

BENEFITS: Emotional Expression & Regulation, Mind–Body Connection

MATERIALS: Paper and coloring materials

1. Explain feelings using the following weather metaphor:

   We all feel different things. Sometimes we feel dark and stormy, and sometimes we feel bright and sunny. Sometimes we feel partly sunny and other times we have rain in the morning and sun in the afternoon. All our feelings are welcome and okay. Our feelings do not make us good or bad. They are information that helps us understand what we need.

2. Have your child use the paper and coloring materials to create a drawing that shows the type of weather they are feeling at the moment. Anything goes; there is no wrong way to do this.

3. After your child has created their weather report drawing, follow up with them throughout the day to see if anything has changed.

KEEP PLAYING: Use this activity when your child gets home from school to reflect on and communicate how they are feeling about their day. Sometimes talking directly about how we feel is hard, and it feels easier to explain our feelings in an artistic way.

Body Investigator

Learning how to connect to the sensations within our physical body is a challenge for anyone at any age. This is an important skill, because these sensations can help us determine our needs, both physical and emotional. Mindfulness helps us notice these sensations in the moment and work toward identifying how to use them as information. This activity offers a simple and playful metaphor to explain this idea to children.

BENEFITS: Mind–Body Connection, Emotional Expression & Regulation

MATERIALS: Paper and coloring materials

1. Start by explaining the metaphor:

    Imagine there is a teeny-tiny body investigator that lives inside our body. This investigator's job is to help us figure out how our body feels. Our body has sensations that tell us how we feel, like cold, hot, or hungry. We also have sensations when we have emotions. Like when we get nervous, we might get sweaty. We can ask our body investigator to help us understand how our body feels so we know what we need.

2. Have your child use the art materials and their imagination to draw what they think their body investigator looks like. Anything goes!

3. Once they have a drawing of their body investigator, continue the metaphor:

    Our body investigator has different modes that they can turn on or off. Sometimes our investigator is in "silent mode" and we don't really know what our sensations are or what we need. Other times we can ask our investigator to activate "notice mode" so they can help us really notice what is happening in the moment and what we need!

4. Have your child spend some time practicing asking their body investigator to turn on "notice mode" by simply saying, *Activate notice mode!*

5. Once your child has activated "notice mode," have them scan their body and identify a sensation somewhere. It can be simple, like the sensation of their legs on the chair, or more complicated, like the way their stomach feels inside.

6. Encourage your child to use specific words to describe the sensations, such as *hot, tight, sharp, dull, stiff, frozen,* or *tingly.*

MASTER MINDFULNESS TIP: The more you talk about this metaphor, the easier it will be for your child to notice their sensations. Ask them to *activate "notice mode"* at different times throughout the day to try to find out how their body feels.

Thought Boats

One playful way to increase a child's understanding of mindfulness is by creating something concrete and tangible. Mindfulness concepts are generally abstract, making them hard for a child to comprehend. This activity will help your child understand the mindfulness practice of noticing thoughts without getting carried away by them.

BENEFITS: **Self-Compassion & Confidence, Emotional Expression & Regulation**

MATERIALS: **Small pieces of paper such as sticky notes, pens, objects that can hold small pieces of paper and can float (like small cups, bowls, plastic bottle caps, or small floating bath toys), large plastic container**

1. Ask your child to describe thoughts they have had in the past or are having right now. Write these thoughts down on small pieces of paper. Crumple each thought paper into a small ball.

2. Have your child choose some small objects that can float to be their thought boats. Place the crumpled balls of paper in the boats.

3. Fill the plastic container with water. Place the thought boats in the water.

4. Explain the metaphor with the following script:

   Our minds can be just like this water, filled up with many different thoughts, like these thought boats floating around. When we are mindful, we try to see all our thoughts but not get carried away by them. We can see they are there, but we don't have to do anything about them or try to get rid of them.

5. Take turns taking deep breaths and blowing the thought boats around the water.

MASTER MINDFULNESS TIP: **As your child blows the thought boats around the water, have them try to notice the boats without guessing or trying to remember what thought each one is carrying.**

I Am a Tree

An amazing way to practice mindfulness with children is by helping them learn how to visualize in their mind. One simple and developmentally appropriate way to do this is by reading them an imaginative story. Cuddle up together, read to them in your softest voice, and help them foster this powerful skill.

BENEFITS: Creativity & Flexible Thinking, Stress & Anxiety Management, Calm & Relaxation

1. Find a comfortable place to cuddle together.

2. Ask your child to turn on their imagination and consider closing their eyes.

3. Read the following instructions aloud:

    a. *Take a deep breath in.*

    b. *Now imagine in your mind that you are a tree. Pretend you are growing roots down into the ground and branches high into the sky. Imagine what your tree looks like. What color is your bark? Is it soft or bumpy? What type of leaves do you have? What color are they?*

    c. *Imagine how it feels to be so big and so tall! What do you notice being up so high in the sky?*

    d. *Take in another deep breath and open your eyes.*

4. Have your child share what they saw and what it was like being a tree. Some questions you might ask are:

    a. *What did your tree look like?*

    b. *Did your tree have leaves, buds, or flowers?*

    c. *How did it feel to imagine being a tree?*

KEEP PLAYING: Grab some paper and coloring materials and have your child draw a picture of what they saw. This will help them further develop their visualization skills.

Movie Magic

The goal of this activity is to help your child use visualization as a tool to solve a problem. Studies have shown that when we visualize ourselves achieving a challenging task or solving a problem, we are more likely to be successful at doing so in the future.

BENEFITS: Creativity & Flexible Thinking, Executive Functioning Skills

MATERIALS: Paper and coloring materials

1. With your child, identify a problem or challenge that they are experiencing. It can be something small, like finishing their math homework, or something big, like learning to swim.

2. Next, have your child draw a picture of themself overcoming this challenge. It can be as creative or magical as they want! Maybe a fairy comes and helps them finish their math homework, or they develop fins and gills to help them swim. Anything goes!

3. Once they have finished drawing the picture, have them imagine the scene like a movie playing in their mind.

4. Encourage your child to create new drawings and movies, coming up with a different creative way to solve the problem each time.

MASTER MINDFULNESS TIP: Try applying this tool in your own life and notice how it feels to visualize yourself achieving something difficult in different ways.

The Feelings Wave

This activity helps children understand how to actually feel feelings through the use of a simple metaphor. Knowing how to feel our feelings is an important and powerful skill. We all have feelings, and all our feelings are welcome and okay. We are more capable of understanding and tolerating our emotions and the challenges of life when we can learn how to notice our feelings and ride the feelings wave.

BENEFITS: Emotional Expression & Regulation

1. Explain the feelings wave metaphor:

   All of us have feelings, and all our feelings are welcome and okay. We get mad, sad, worried, nervous, happy, excited, and so much more! No feeling stays forever. Our feelings come and go. And guess what? We can learn how to notice our feelings in the moment and ride them just like a surfer riding a wave. When we do this, we actually can change how we are feeling faster! First, we notice our feeling as it begins to rise up. Then we let the feeling stay. Finally, we watch it as it shrinks and drifts away.

2. Now instruct your child on how to ride the wave:

   a. ***Notice the feeling:*** *Find where you feel the feeling in your body. Name where it is and the sensation you feel. For example, you might say I feel a tight feeling in my chest.*

   b. ***Let the feeling stay:*** *Breathe in and out slowly three times. Each time you breathe in, imagine that your breath is going to that place in your body. Don't try to make the feeling change. Just allow it to be there.*

   c. ***Watch the feeling:*** *See how your body sensations and emotions change after a few breaths.*

3. Have your child ride the feelings wave as many times as they need, until the emotion feels like something they can handle!

MASTER MINDFULNESS TIP: This is a great tool for you to use as well when you are feeling overwhelmed by your child. Riding the feelings wave can help you shift out of dysregulation and into a calm and grounded place.

My Favorite Color

This activity helps build on a child's skill of visualization through simple guided imagery. Finding a comfortable seat, breathing, and focusing the mind on one thing is a great way for anyone to practice mindfulness.

BENEFITS: Creativity & Flexible Thinking, Stress & Anxiety Management, Calm & Relaxation

1. Find a comfortable place to cuddle together.

2. Ask your child to turn on their imagination and consider closing their eyes.

3. Read the following directions aloud:

   a. *Take a deep breath in through your nose. Breathe it out through your mouth, making an AHH sound.*

   b. *Imagine that the air around you can be seen and it is your favorite color. Imagine that this colored air is filled with things that make you feel happy, calm, strong, and safe. Every time you breathe in, you are filling up with this colored air and whatever good things you want.*

   c. *Let's take five or six deep breaths together, filling up with as much colored air as we can.*

4. Have your child share what color they imagined. Questions you might ask include:

   a. *What good things did you imagine?*

   b. *How did your favorite color make you feel?*

MASTER MINDFULNESS TIP: This is a great activity to do before bed to help your child find calm and relaxation before falling asleep.

Imagine a World

Sometimes we feel overwhelmed by something that is happening in our life. Children can feel more capable of overcoming something challenging when they have play experiences that make them feel powerful. This activity is a playful way for children to feel big and strong.

BENEFITS: Self-Compassion & Confidence, Creativity & Flexible Thinking

MATERIALS: Paper, coloring materials, blocks, Magna-Tiles, people figurines, Legos

1. Explain that you are going to create an imaginary world together. In this world, anything can happen. Any type of magic, special powers, superheroes, or mythical creatures can be there!

2. Use any type of material you have on hand or that your child prefers to create this world. Use blocks or Legos to build a world you can both interact with, or use paper and markers to draw different parts of the world.

3. Once the world has been created, work together to make up a story about it. Ask your child questions such as:

   a. *Who lives in this world?*

   b. *What types of problems are here?*

   c. *If something goes wrong, who can come and fix it?*

4. Notice out loud as your child creates, saying things like *This world is filled with so many protectors!* Sit with them at their eye level and follow their lead.

MASTER MINDFULNESS TIP: After the activity is completed, close your eyes, have your child close theirs, and imagine the world together. See if you can describe different things about the world to each other.

Animal Sidekick

The goal of this activity is to help your child create an internal sense of confidence. Tapping into creativity and imagination through visualization is a great way to build up a child's sense of self.

BENEFITS: Creativity & Flexible Thinking, Self-Compassion & Confidence

1. Find a comfortable place to cuddle together.

2. Ask your child to turn on their imagination and consider closing their eyes.

3. Read the following instructions aloud:

    a. *Take a deep breath in, then let it out.*

    b. *Almost every superhero has a sidekick. Let's imagine you have your very own animal sidekick. What type of animal is it? Is it big or small? Does it have fur or scales? Is it a real animal or an imaginary one? How do you communicate with your sidekick?*

    c. *Imagine that you and your sidekick are together, ready to take on the world! How does it feel, knowing that you can do it together?*

    d. *Take a deep breath in, then let it out. Open your eyes when you are ready.*

4. Have your child share what they imagined and what it was like having this animal sidekick.

KEEP PLAYING: Have your child create a drawing of their animal sidekick. Prompt them to imagine a situation in the future when their sidekick could help them out.

Stuffy Talks

Often it can be hard for a child to verbalize how they are feeling or what an experience was like for them. Using play or fun props is a great way to help a child communicate. This activity uses stuffed animals to allow children to talk about how they feel without actually having to describe what they are feeling.

BENEFITS: Emotional Expression & Regulation, Creativity & Flexible Thinking, Parent/Caregiver–Child Connection

MATERIALS: Stuffed animals

1. Pick out a few stuffed animals.

2. You and your child are going to communicate using the stuffed animals. You can pretend that the animals can talk or that you can read their minds and speak for them.

3. Have the stuffed animals ask each other questions. The conversation can be about anything. For example, if your child is worried or scared about an upcoming event, have one stuffed animal ask another how it feels about the upcoming event. This might sound something like *Bunny, I heard you are about to go to a new school. How do you feel about that?*

4. Keep the conversation going for as long as your child is engaged or as long as it feels good.

KEEP PLAYING: If you talked about an upcoming event of concern, bring the stuffed animal that seemed to "speak" for your child to the event. Playfully check in with that stuffed animal along the way.

Ceiling Watch

Lying on our back with our feet up against a wall is a great way to soothe the body and calm the nervous system. You can turn this body position into an opportunity for imagination and playfulness, which can strengthen a joyful, mindful connection between you and your child.

BENEFITS: Calm & Relaxation, Parent/Caregiver–Child Connection, Creativity & Flexible Thinking

1. Find a comfortable and accessible way for you and your child to lie on your backs near a wall. Slowly walk your feet up the wall until your legs are stretched out comfortably, with the soles of your feet facing the ceiling. If this position feels uncomfortable, you or your child may choose to lie on the floor with feet resting on a couch, chair, or bed.

2. Prompt your child to use their imagination and pretend that the ceiling is a window to another world.

3. Working together, try to imagine all the different things you can see. Ask your child questions about this world, such as:

    a. *What do you see? (trees, water, or even a mountain made of candy?)*

    b. *What kinds of things are there? (animals, people, fairies, superheroes?)*

    c. *What is the weather like?*

4. Stay in this position for about three to five minutes as you talk about this world.

MASTER MINDFULNESS TIP: Don't forget to take deep breaths! Try to take three to five deep breaths together at the start and end of the activity.

Magic Carpet Ride

The goal of this activity is to help your child find calm through mindful imagination. Lead them through this fun and simple guided visualization to boost their mindfulness skills.

BENEFITS: Creativity & Flexible Thinking, Stress & Anxiety Management, Calm & Relaxation

1. Find a comfortable place to cuddle together.

2. Ask your child to turn on their imagination and consider closing their eyes.

3. Read the following instructions aloud:

   a. *Breathe gently in and out*

   b. *Imagine that underneath you is a colorful magic carpet. It is beautiful, filled with color, love, and safety. Imagine you are touching the carpet. It is soft and cozy, and just the right size for you!*

   c. *Your carpet begins to fly, taking you high into the sky, flying you gently through the soft pillowy clouds. You feel free, light, and calm. You begin to notice that your worries, troubles, and problems are being left among the clouds. You continue to soar through the sky!*

   d. *When you are ready to land, take a deep breath in and glide your magic carpet to the ground.*

4. Have your child share what they saw and how they feel after their magic carpet ride.

MASTER MINDFULNESS TIP: This is a great activity to do before bed or after school just before a child starts their homework.

Sticky Thoughts

The goal of this activity is to help your child imagine changing their mood. Although all feelings are considered neutral, meaning it is best not to label them good or bad, we can benefit from working to change certain moods. For example, worries can sometimes feel "sticky," like we can't get away from them. This activity is a playful way to help your child identify a worry and work to get unstuck from it.

BENEFITS: Emotional Expression & Regulation, Calm & Relaxation

MATERIALS: Bubble liquid (optional)

1. Explain that all of us have worries, and sometimes our worries can feel sticky, as if they are stuck in our brain and we can't get rid of them.

2. Explain that our breath is so powerful, it can help us send the stuck worry away.

3. Next, you and your child will each pick something you feel worried about.

4. It is time to unstick those thoughts. Walk your child through the following steps (have bubble liquid prepped and ready, if using):

   a. *Say out loud the worry that is stuck. (For example, I'm worried about going to the doctor.)*

   b. *Take a deep breath in. This breath will find the stuck worry.*

   c. *Let out the breath and blow the worry into a bubble (real or imagined).*

   d. *Watch the bubble carry your worry away.*

MASTER MINDFULNESS TIP: If using real bubbles, have your child practice being in the present moment by seeing if they can hear the bubbles popping.

CHAPTER 7

Grounding Games

The more that children experience challenges through games and play, the more capable they become at handling challenges in real life. The activities in this chapter are intended to help children practice their ability to focus and overcome challenges. In addition, children will grow their self-control and resilience. Mindfulness is a powerful tool that can help anyone learn how to improve attention and focus in the moment. It can also help us build self-compassion and acceptance in the face of obstacles. The activities in this chapter will help your child intertwine mindfulness, focus, and challenging play in a powerful way.

Focused Tree

We build focus and confidence when we do something that is both physically challenging and mentally challenging. This activity will require you and your child to do both!

BENEFITS: Focus & Attention, Self-Compassion & Confidence, Grounding & Coping Skills, Impulse Control

1. Pick one of you to be a tree and the other the wind.

2. The person who is the tree will stand in Tree Pose (see step 3), trying not to fall out of the pose. Set limits around safety: The wind person is not allowed to push, kick, or physically use their body get the tree person to fall.

3. For the Tree Pose, begin in a standing position. Lift one foot and place the heel against the opposite ankle, with toes touching the ground. With a strong belly, push fists together in front of the heart or reach arms to the sky.

4. The person who is the wind will try to distract the tree person by doing silly dance moves, making funny sounds, or even pretending that they are blowing a strong wind toward the tree.

5. Once the wind has knocked down the tree, switch roles.

MASTER MINDFULNESS TIP: For an added challenge, make a rule that the wind can't make any noise. You both must stay silent as the wind tries to distract the tree.

Wiggle, Jump, Freeze, Walk

The goal of this activity is to help your child experience challenge in a playful way. When we can do something challenging, we learn to believe that we can do other difficult things, too. Having this mindset can help improve your child's self-esteem and sense of self.

BENEFITS: Focus & Attention, Self-Compassion & Confidence, Impulse Control

1. Choose one of you to be the leader and the other the follower.
2. The leader will call out at least two actions, such as *walk* and *freeze*.
3. For the first round, the follower tries to do the action that the leader calls out.
4. For the second round, the goal will be for the follower to do the opposite action of what the leader calls out:
   - Wiggle means Freeze
   - Freeze means Wiggle
5. After a few rounds, switch roles.

KEEP PLAYING: Have your child make up other actions to do together and opposite of each other. They can be as silly or serious as they like!

Positive Tapping Fingers

One great way to help your child focus and find calm is by pairing movements with positive statements. This activity creates a connection between positive thoughts, or affirmations, and simple hand movements, which can help your child feel more grounded, calm, and focused.

BENEFITS: Focus & Attention, Self-Compassion & Confidence

1. Work together to pick a four-syllable positive phrase, something that you would like your child to believe about themself; for example, *I am worth it* or *I can do it*.

2. Once you have the phrase, it's time to tap! Using both hands, demonstrate the following steps for your child:

   - Press your index finger into your thumb as you say *I*.
   - Press your middle finger into your thumb as you say *am*.
   - Press your ring finger into your thumb as you say *worth*.
   - Press your pinkie finger into your thumb as you say *it*.

3. Now ask your child to copy your movements.

4. Have your child repeat the positive statement and finger tapping one time out loud, one time in a whisper voice, and one time silently in their mind.

MASTER MINDFULNESS TIP: This is a great activity to run through before your child is about to do something hard. Do a quick round of finger tapping to build focus and confidence.

Word Focus

This activity combines focused attention and internal awareness. It can be hard to pay attention to things happening around us as well as inside of us at the same time. This game will work to help your child notice the present moment, both internally and externally.

BENEFITS: Focus & Attention, Mind–Body Connection, Present-Moment Awareness

1. Have your child find a comfortable seated position.

2. Tell your child that they are be going to be noticing what is happening inside their body when they hear different words. Words can make them experience different sensations and feelings. If they are not sure how to notice, suggest they ask their body investigator to *activate "notice mode"* (see Body Investigator activity on page 66).

3. With your child seated comfortably, ask them to consider closing their eyes as you read the following words out loud to them. Pause briefly after each word (add, leave out, or change words depending on your child's age):

   - *Birthday*
   - *Snow*
   - *Homework*
   - *Thunderstorm*
   - *Trouble*
   - *Cake*
   - *Puppy*
   - *Bear*

4. Have your child open their eyes and share what they noticed in their body when they heard the different words.

KEEP PLAYING: Switch roles! Have your child say any words they want out loud as you sit with eyes closed. Notice how it feels in your body as you hear these words.

Body Check

This activity is a challenging way for your child to practice present-moment awareness. When we put our body in motion, it can be hard to pause and notice it. During this game, your child will be working to build their awareness even during moments of silliness.

BENEFITS: Focus & Attention, Mind–Body Connection

1. Explain that you will both move your bodies in a crazy way, like dancing to music, jumping, running, or spinning.

2. You will move in this silly way until one of you yells out, *Body check.*

3. Body check means you both freeze, then try to notice and call out one feeling or sensation in your body. This might sound like *I feel my feet on the carpet* or *My legs feel wiggly.* You should each try to describe only one thing. Really notice it!

4. After the body check, start moving again. But this time, see if you can each notice the sensation from the first check as you move.

5. Every time you do a body check, see if your child can list all the different things they noticed before, adding one each time!

MASTER MINDFULNESS TIP: Encourage your child to try to use descriptive words during the body check, such as hot, cold, fuzzy, sticky, burning, wiggly, and frozen, to name a few.

Morning Hunt

Getting our children ready and out of the house in the morning can sometimes be challenging and stressful. Using mindfulness during everyday tasks can add a bit of excitement and surprise and, in turn, create the opportunity for your child to be more engaged and agreeable.

BENEFITS: Focus & Attention, Executive Functioning Skills

MATERIALS: Clothes, timer, backpack, hairbrush

1. Explain that the goal of this activity is for your child to find hidden items and put them on before time runs out.

2. Choose the items you want your child to search for and hide them. Depending on the time available and your child's age, make the hiding spots obvious or challenging, or limit the number of items you hide. For example, you could hide your child's pants, shirt, and socks, or just their hairbrush or backpack.

3. Set the timer to a reasonable number, given the task and amount of time you have. Two or three minutes is usually enough.

4. Help your child notice what is around them and remind them what they are looking for. You might say, *We are hunting for your socks. Do you think we can find them before the time runs out?*

5. Praise your child for using their awareness skills as they find each item!

MASTER MINDFULNESS TIP: Use the classic clue of hot or cold to help your child get a sense of how close they are to finding an item as they look.

Bathmat Mindfulness

This activity will help your child practice being still. Sitting still and noticing our body and breath is an advanced skill, but it's one worth practicing, because it is beneficial for both the body and mind.

BENEFITS: Focus & Attention, Calm & Relaxation, Grounding & Coping Skills

MATERIALS: Small bathmat, rug, blanket, pillow or towel

1. Choose a small item that your child can use as their mindfulness mat. It should be something that they can access at any time and is comfortable to sit on.

2. Have them choose a place to put their mat. Explain this is a special place for them to sit and no one else.

3. Explain the purpose of the mindfulness mat:

   As soon as you sit on this mat, you become a master of mindfulness. On this mat, you can practice sitting still and breathing. It sounds simple, but it's actually pretty hard. It's something only a mindfulness master can do. Do you want to try?

4. Have your child sit comfortably on the mat. Guide them to place one hand on their belly and the other hand on their heart.

5. Take three to five deep breaths together, trying to notice just the breath in the moment.

6. Encourage your child to spend time being a mindfulness master anytime they want!

MASTER MINDFULNESS TIP: This is a great activity to try in the morning after your child wakes up or right before bed.

Mindful Hockey

This activity is a spin on a classic family therapy game. Throughout this game, you will be working together to stay focused, connected, and calm. Practicing these skills will help you both find these qualities in moments of overwhelm.

BENEFITS: Focus & Attention, Parent/Caregiver–Child Connection, Calm & Relaxation

MATERIALS: Cotton Balls

1. Sit at a table together, facing each other and close enough that your hands and arms can touch.

2. Place a cotton ball on the table, between you, to act as a hockey puck.

3. Gently wrap your hands around your child's wrists or arms. Have your child do the same with your wrists or arms. Together, your arms should form a small rectangle shape. This is your hockey rink!

4. In silence, using just your breath and eye contact, pass the "puck" back and forth across the "rink."

5. Try to move the puck back and forth between you five times!

MASTER MINDFULNESS TIP: Encourage your child to try to keep their mind focused on only their breath and the puck, paying attention on purpose to only those two things.

Focused Balance

A great way to build focus and present-moment awareness is by working through a physical challenge. This fun activity creates an opportunity for you and your child to connect as you work through this balancing challenge.

BENEFITS: Parent/Caregiver–Child Connection, Focus & Attention, Present-Moment Awareness

MATERIALS: Pillows

1. Start by explaining that the child is going to be working on building their focus and attention by trying to stand balanced on pillows.

2. Start with one or two pillows. It's best to start small and add as you go!

3. Help the child stand on the pillows by holding their hands or by hugging them around the waist.

4. Once they are steady enough, remove your hands briefly, letting them practice balancing on their own.

5. After they practice a few times, let them jump into your arms.

MASTER MINDFULNESS TIP: Try taking deep, slow breaths while they find their balance, to see if they can balance longer.

Camera Eyes

The goal of this activity is to increase your child's attention and focus in the present moment. When we exercise our memory and attention to detail, we are building our attention span and ability to be present.

BENEFITS: Executive Functioning Skills, Focus & Attention, Impulse Control

MATERIALS: 6 to 10 small objects or toys, blanket

1. Arrange the small toys or objects in a group.

2. Explain to your child they are going to take a picture of the objects with their eyes. Allow them about a minute to study the objects and take a photo in their mind.

3. Cover the objects with a blanket or have your child simply close their eyes. Remove one object from the group and place it out of view.

4. Remove the blanket and have your child try to guess which object has been removed.

5. Repeat until all the objects have been removed.

KEEP PLAYING: Place the objects in a specific order and have your child take a photo in their mind. Then change the order and ask your child to try to recall what order the objects were in.

Back Art

This is another classic family therapy game that has been given a mindfulness twist. This activity works to build connection, focus, and present-moment awareness between you and your child. Using healthy touch is a great way to create a playful connection between the two of you.

BENEFITS: Parent/Caregiver–Child Connection, Focus & Attention, Present-Moment Awareness

1. Decide who is going to be the artist and who is going to be the canvas.

2. The artist is going to use their finger to draw a simple picture on the other person's back, pretending it is a canvas.

3. The canvas needs to pay close attention to the sensations they feel on their back to help them figure out what the artist is drawing.

4. Once the artist has completed the drawing, the canvas tries to guess what they drew!

5. Take turns being the artist and being the canvas.

MASTER MINDFULNESS TIP: If you have already played Body Investigator (page 66), encourage your child to *activate "notice mode"* to cue their mind to build connections to the physical sensations on their back.

Sunshine and Snow Clouds

This activity teaches children how to use progressive muscle relaxation, which is a technique commonly used to relax the nervous system. It involves being able to match a specific body movement (tense or relax) to a verbal instruction, which takes a lot of focus. This is an amazing way to calm the body and mind and practice focus and concentration skills all at the same time.

BENEFITS: Focus & Attention, Mind–Body Connection, Calm & Relaxation

1. Explain to your child that you will be working to tense and relax different muscles in their body at different times.

2. Next, explain "tense" versus "relax," as follows:

   When we make our muscles tense, we take a deep breath in and squeeze our muscles, making them hard and tight, almost like they are frozen. When we relax our muscles, we breathe out and make our muscles loose, almost like they are melting ice.

3. Show your child how to do this by modeling how you tense up and relax your feet or your hands as you inhale and exhale.

4. Explain that for this game when you say *Snow clouds on your (insert body part here),* your child should try to make that part of their body tense by squeezing their muscles really tight (to no more than a count of three).

5. When you say *Sunshine on your (insert body part here),* they should attempt to relax their muscles, trying to make them loose and soft, like melting ice.

6. Work together to find a comfortable position for this activity. This could be sitting or standing.

7. Take turns saying where the snow clouds are (which body part) and where the sunshine is. Try to move through the whole body.

MASTER MINDFULNESS TIP: The activity becomes even more beneficial if you match the inhale with snow clouds and the exhale with sunshine. This is a great activity for your child to practice matching their breath with subtle body movement.

Pass the Story

This classic game is a great way for children to expand their focus, attention, and creativity. For this activity, you and your child will take turns telling parts of a story. The most important aspect of the game is that you must repeat what the storyteller said before you! This game helps us engage our memory and practice paying attention to the present moment.

BENEFITS: Focus & Attention, Creativity & Flexible Thinking

1. Decide who is going to start the story. The person who starts tells two or three sentences of a story. Anything goes! The only rule is that the storylines can't be from a book, show, or video game—they must be made up by the storyteller.

2. Once the first storyteller has shared their lines, they pass the story on. Then the second storyteller begins. But before the second storyteller can add to the story, they must repeat what the first storyteller said.

3. Continue to pass the story back and forth until one of you leaves out a part or the story becomes too long to remember!

KEEP PLAYING: This is a great game to play in the car! So many times, we can get caught in a pattern of asking our children the same questions about their day. This game takes the pressure off but still supports a connection.

Human GPS

Inspired by Deborah Plummer's book *Focusing and Calming Games for Children,* this challenging activity develops the skill of focused attention by encouraging children to use only one sense at a time. When your child practices challenging activities in a playful way, they become better at problem-solving. This is an advanced skill. If you feel that your child isn't ready for it just yet, come back to this activity later.

BENEFITS: **Creativity & Flexible Thinking, Focus & Attention, Present-Moment Awareness, Mind–Body Connection**

MATERIALS: **Masking or painter's tape, blankets or pillows, blindfold (optional)**

1. Find a safe indoor environment. Using tape or blankets and pillows, create a path or road through the space, with a starting point and an ending point. (Note: If you are using blankets or pillows, you will not be walking on them but trying to walk around them. If you are using tape, you will be walking on the tape.)

2. Choose one person to be the GPS and one person to be the car. Explain that a GPS is a special type of electronic map that we can use to go from place to place. If you are the car, you will try to follow the path using only your sense of hearing. You can be blindfolded or just close your eyes.

3. The person who is the GPS will be giving directions to the car without using words like *Turn left* or *Go straight ahead*. Instead, the GPS will give directions by using different sounds, such as chirping like a bird to indicate turning left and barking like a dog to indicate turning right.

4. Before the car starts along the path, make sure it is clear what sounds the GPS will be using to signal the different directions the car can go.

5. Now the car begins its journey. The goal is for the car to make it all the way along the path and arrive at the ending point by only following the agreed-upon GPS directions.

6. Take turns being the GPS and the car.

KEEP PLAYING: **Try a variation of this game where the car watches the GPS do different movements, such as clapping or hopping on one foot, to indicate different directions instead of making sounds.**

CHAPTER 8

Mindful Art & Music

The activities in this chapter use music and art as avenues for you and your child to experiment with mindfulness. Music is a powerful tool for teaching children, thanks to its grounding and soothing abilities. In addition, children are often more likely to remember a skill or be willing to practice a new task when they can do it in a creative way. Along with ways to use music mindfully, this chapter offers developmentally appropriate ways for your child to experience mindfulness through art. Art creates amazing sensory input for our bodies and is a great way for children to tune in to their experiences in the present moment.

Notice Mind

The goal of this activity is to weave mindfulness into your child's daily routine. Singing a song with a playful connection to an ordinary task is a great way to turn that task into a mindful moment.

BENEFITS: Parent/Caregiver–Child Connection, Present-Moment Awareness

1. Explain to your child that you will be working together to turn on their "notice mind." You could say:

   Our "notice mind" helps us pay attention to one thing at a time. When you are trying to put your shoes on and get outside for the bus, your mind can be focused on many different things. Our notice mind helps us stop and focus on the thing we need to do right now.

2. Sing the following song, to the tune of "Are You Sleeping (Brother John)?" or say it as a chant to help your child focus on what they are doing in the moment (these lyrics are only an example):

   Turn on notice mind, turn on notice mind, we're noticing our feet, we're noticing out feet. So we can get our shoes on, so we can go to school. Notice mind, notice mind.

3. Use this song to cue your child to bring their attention to the present moment and focus on the task at hand.

MASTER MINDFULNESS TIP: This is a great activity to use when you are on the verge of overwhelm. Singing is an effective way to regulate our nervous system and decrease the chance of our yelling or saying things we will regret later.

Artistic Focus

This activity can help your child increase their focus and attention to detail. One of the key aspects of mindfulness is being present in the moment. The world around us is filled with distractions, making focused attention challenging at times. This activity is a simple, artistic way to help your child foster this skill.

BENEFITS: Focus & Attention, Impulse Control

MATERIALS: Paper, drawing materials, toy or other object

1. Help your child choose an object to look at with an artist's eyes. Any object will do, like a toy, a stuffed animal, or even a stick.

2. Explain that they will be using their artist eyes to really focus on the object, carefully studying it and trying to notice every small detail of it.

3. Give them a few minutes to study the object.

4. Now have your child attempt to draw the object in detail, using their best artistic skills.

MASTER MINDFULNESS TIP: To increase the level of challenge and focus, remove the object after your child has studied it and have them try to draw it in detail from memory.

Scribble Thoughts

The goal of this activity is to give your child the opportunity to manage difficult emotions without talking about them. Sometimes it is hard to explain how we feel or talk about a worry we have. This activity uses art to create a safe and effective way for your child to express their stressors on the page and scribble them away.

BENEFITS: Emotional Expression & Regulation, Calm & Relaxation, Stress & Anxiety Management, Creativity & Flexible Thinking

MATERIALS: Several pieces of paper and coloring materials, or a dry-erase board and markers

1. With your child, identify a current or upcoming stressor. For example, maybe they feel angry that they can't play video games right now or are worried about a test.

2. Explain they are going to notice what they are thinking and feeling, but they don't have to talk about it.

3. Ask them to draw something to represent the feelings they are having about this current or upcoming stressor. They can draw whatever they like—pictures, lines, words, people, or color blotches. Be sure to say something like *There are no "supposed tos." Just draw whatever you want, even if it doesn't make sense.*

4. Once they finish their drawing, have them scribble over the whole picture using a dark colored pencil or marker. Encourage them to scribble fast, going back and forth over the picture. Have them scribble until they can no longer see what they drew. When they have finished, ask them to take a mindful breath with you.

5. Now, on a new piece of paper, have them draw something else that represents how the stressor is making them feel. (If using a dry-erase board, simply erase the first image.) As before, they can draw whatever they like. Be sure to repeat that *There are no supposed tos.*

6. Once the drawing is finished, have them repeat the scribbling described in step 4. Again, breathe together when they are done scribbling.

7. Repeat the drawing and scribbling steps as many times as your child would like, always remembering to breathe together at the end.

8. When your child feels they are done drawing and scribbling for this stressor, have them *activate "notice mode"* or connect with their body investigator (page 66) to see if their feelings have stayed the same or changed in any way.

MASTER MINDFULNESS TIP: This is a great activity for processing a stressor the whole family is experiencing. Doing the steps together and working on your own emotions related to an experience is a great way to create connection and model healthy emotion regulation.

Mantra Stone

A mantra is a repeated phrase or sound used to help focus the mind. We can use a mantra like a catchphrase to bring attention to a particular feeling or idea. In this activity, you and your child will create a personal catchphrase and a visual representation of it.

BENEFITS: Focus & Attention, Calm & Relaxation, Self-Compassion & Confidence

MATERIALS: Stone or rock, paint, markers, glitter glue

1. Help your child find a stone or rock outside that is suitable for painting (or purchase one at a craft store).

2. Next, work together to create a mantra or catchphrase that your child can say to themselves. It can be a statement about them or something they are working toward. It might be an "I" statement, like *I can do it, I am brave,* or *I am worth it.* Or it could be a single word, like *focus, breathe,* or *smile.*

3. Instruct your child to decorate the rock to represent their mantra, using various art materials. They might wish to write the mantra on the stone or just decorate the stone to represent it. Encourage them to let their creativity run loose!

4. Create as many mantras and stones as your child would like.

MASTER MINDFULNESS TIP: Have your child use their mantra stone during Bath-mat Mindfulness (page 88) as a way to build focus and attention. Instruct them to hold the stone in their hand and repeat the mantra as they notice their breath.

The Inside Me

One of the many benefits of mindfulness is that it helps us develop a better understanding of our thoughts, sensations, and internal experiences. Many times, we have a version of ourselves inside us that we keep hidden or don't always show the people around us. This activity uses a physical box to help your child explore how their internal experiences and emotions might be different from what they show on the outside.

BENEFITS: Mind–Body Connection, Emotional Expression & Regulation

MATERIALS: Small box of any kind, coloring materials, paint, glitter, glue, small craft items (such as beads, sequins, stickers, googly eyes), magazines

1. Explain the idea of "inside me" to your child. You might say something like:

   Sometimes we have thoughts, feelings, and sensations inside us that we don't let other people know about. We might be feeling scared, worried, or angry about something on the inside, but we look happy and calm on the outside. Sometimes we might not want other people to know our "inside me." But it's okay to notice our inside thoughts and feelings and share them with someone we trust.

2. Help your child express and create their own idea of "inside me" using the box. The inside of the box will represent the things they often think, feel, and notice on the inside that they don't always show. They can draw or paint inside the box, or glue pictures from magazines or small craft items on it.

3. Instruct your child to use the outside of the box to represent what everyone sees about them on the outside.

4. Once they've completed their box, your child can fill it with different items that feel special or important to them.

MASTER MINDFULNESS TIP: Don't push your child to explain anything about their "inside me." Allow them to notice and share only what they want. This activity is about them building their own self-awareness, not an opportunity for you to get an inside scoop.

I Am Unique

A great way to help your child build self-confidence is by bringing awareness to the things you notice about them. Sometimes the rush of life can get in the way of our slowing down and really noticing all the wonderful attributes our child has. This activity is a powerful and simple way to boost their confidence and strengthen your connection with them!

BENEFITS: Parent/Caregiver–Child Connection, Self-Compassion & Confidence

MATERIALS: Paper, writing materials

1. Draw a large outline of a face to represent your child.

2. In the face area, write as many wonderful and special things about your child as you can think of. You can write character traits, such as *loving*, *brave*, *caring*, or *silly*, as well as special skills they have, like *great writer* or *tennis player*. Try to fill the whole area with unique and special things about them.

3. When you are done, read what you have written out loud to them.

KEEP PLAYING: A great way to increase your connection during this activity is by having your child snuggle up with you as you read aloud from the page. You can elaborate on what you wrote by giving examples of times you noticed these things about them.

Feel My Feelings

Learning how to feel our feelings can be complicated for both adults and children. This activity uses art to help your child explore and express different emotions. By thinking about where those emotions are felt in their body, they can develop greater emotional awareness.

BENEFITS: Emotional Expression & Regulation, Mind–Body Connection, Stress & Anxiety Management

MATERIALS: Paper and coloring materials

1. Explain to your child that when we have different emotions, like happy or mad, we also have different sensations in our bodies. For example, when some people get worried, they get a stomachache. Remind your child that they can ask their body investigator (page 66) to *activate "notice mode"* to help them understand how something feels.

2. Pick a feeling to notice, like happy, mad, or worried. Using the art materials, have them create an image to represent how it feels in their body when they are feeling this way.

3. Ask questions as they create to help guide them to notice their body. For example: *Do you feel that feeling in your stomach or maybe in your arms?* You can also build a connection by telling them where you notice that feeling in your body. For example: *When I am sad, I get a tight feeling in my throat.*

KEEP PLAYING: After doing this activity, ask your child about how their body feels when they are experiencing different emotions. You can even model by saying how your body is feeling in that moment.

Music Mind

This activity is a simple way to add mindfulness to your child's daily routine. This game uses music to help your child build focused attention to the present moment, a powerful mindfulness skill.

BENEFITS: Focus & Attention, Present-Moment Awareness, Mind–Body Connection

MATERIALS: Music

1. Explain that you are going to play a song, and you will both try to notice certain things during the song. Pick one instrument or sound in the song that you are going to notice. For example, you can choose drums, guitar, or another instrument, or a certain word.

2. Together, come up with a sign, like a thumbs-up or a silly dance move, that each of you will use to indicate that you have heard the chosen sound.

3. Next, decide if this is going to be a competitive or collaborative activity.

4. If you are making it competitive, each person earns a point every time they notice the agreed-upon sound first. The person with the most points at the end of the song wins!

5. If you are playing collaboratively, you should both just try to notice the sound throughout the song, with focused attention.

KEEP PLAYING: This is a great game to play in the car. Listening to music in the car is a fairly common practice, and this is a simple way to add a dash of mindfulness.

Mindful Dance

One of the most powerful ways to build mindfulness is to simply add mindful awareness to things we already do with our children. This activity provides simple, mindfulness-based questions you can ask your child as you dance together.

BENEFITS: Mind–Body Connection, Focus & Attention, Emotional Expression & Regulation

MATERIALS: Music

1. Put on music that would be appropriate for you and your child to dance to.

2. Begin by just listening to the music together, then start to move your bodies slowly.

3. As you move your bodies to the music, ask your child questions, such as:

   a. *How does this song make you feel?*

   b. *How does your body feel when you dance?*

   c. *Can you notice how your feet feel on the ground as you move?*

   d. *Is your breathing faster or slower now that we are dancing?*

4. Continue to ask questions as you dance to each song. Prompt your child to notice how their feelings change from song to song.

MASTER MINDFULNESS TIP: See if you and your child can match your breath to your dance moves, which will help you be more in the present moment.

Messy Art

Different types of messy play, like finger painting, are an amazing way for children to explore physical sensations and be present in the moment. Although the cleanup can sometimes be a pain, the benefit for your child to build present-moment awareness and playful connection can be worth it.

BENEFITS: Present-Moment Awareness, Mind–Body Connection

MATERIALS: Cardboard or muffin tin, nontoxic tempera or finger paint, paper, tablecloth, art smock

1. Fill an old muffin tin with different paints for your child to use as a palette. Alternatively, you could put blobs of paint on a thick piece of cardboard. Nontoxic tempera paint works great.

2. Cover a kid-friendly surface with paper, then let your child get creative. Encourage them to mix colors, get messy, and be in the moment!

3. As they paint and create, ask them these mindfulness questions:

    a. *How does the paint feel on your fingers?*

    b. *Is the paint warm or cold when you touch it?*

    c. *Do you notice the way it smells?*

    d. *How does it feel when you move the paint around on the paper?*

KEEP PLAYING: If your child doesn't enjoy immersive sensory activities, try using a paintbrush and apply small amounts of paint onto their hands, asking them the same mindfulness questions.

Sound Vibrations

Whenever we speak, sing, or hum, we create sound vibrations within our bodies. This activity is a simple and playful way to help your child notice how their body feels when they create sound vibrations by humming.

BENEFITS: Mind–Body Connection, Focus & Attention, Calm & Relaxation

1. Ask your child if they have ever noticed how their body vibrates inside when they make sounds. Explain that when we speak, sing, or hum, our bodies make sound vibrations.

2. Next, have your child close their eyes, if they are comfortable doing so. Ask them to close their mouth and begin to hum a few different notes.

3. Instruct them to take a mindful breath in. On the exhale, ask them to hum out, trying to notice the vibrations in their body as they hum.

4. Repeat this a few times. Each time, ask your child to try to pinpoint where the vibrations are happening in their body.

MASTER MINDFULNESS TIP: Add a level of connection by gently placing your hands on each other's back or chest and humming together. Notice how the other person's body vibrates gently while they hum.

Kindness Bands

A common practice in mindfulness is learning how to send yourself and others kindness and compassion. Sometimes it can be easy to send loving thoughts to others but much harder to be kind to ourselves. This activity will help your child practice this skill in a concrete way.

BENEFITS: Self-Compassion & Confidence, Focus & Attention

MATERIALS: Beads, string or elastic

1. Explain to your child the importance of thinking kind things about ourselves. For example:

   It can be easy to be kind to others but sometimes really hard to be kind to ourselves. It is easy to forget how amazing we are! When we practice speaking kindly to ourselves, we actually can feel happier and more confident.

2. Cut a piece of string long enough to fit comfortably around your child's wrist. Tie a knot at one end of the string.

3. Ask your child to say a kind thing about themself as they put a bead on the string. Have them say one kind thing for each bead they put on. If they struggle to think of something, help them notice kind things about themself.

4. Once the bracelet is complete, tie it around their wrist. Prompt them to use it as a reminder of how amazing they are!

MASTER MINDFULNESS TIP: If you notice your child is having a challenging day, encourage them to look at the bracelet and repeat kind thoughts to themself.

Trash Mind

Our minds can get filled up with a ton of thoughts, feelings, and ideas. Sometimes it gets so filled up, we can't think! The following activity provides a strategy to help your child empty out their mind when they are feeling overwhelmed or scattered.

BENEFITS: Present-Moment Awareness, Focus & Attention, Creativity & Flexible Thinking

MATERIALS: Timer, paper, writing materials

1. Explain to your child that sometimes we have so much going on in our minds, we can't focus. Let them know that they will be using the paper and writing materials to empty out all the thoughts in their mind.

2. Explain that when the timer starts, they will draw, write, scribble, or doodle all the thoughts in their head down on the paper. They can express their thoughts any way they want. Their only goal should be to stay focused on their thoughts and the paper while the timer is going.

3. Decide on an amount of time that feels right for your child, somewhere between three to five minutes.

4. Prompt your child to take a deep breath in and let their thoughts flow as you start the timer.

MASTER MINDFULNESS TIP: This is a great activity to do early in the morning or after a long day before bed.

Worry Bug

Often our worries can become so big, we can't think of anything else. When we can make our worries seem smaller, it can be easier to not get stuck on them. This activity is a great way to help your child when they are struggling with worries.

BENEFITS: Emotional Expression & Regulation, Calm & Relaxation, Stress & Anxiety Management

MATERIALS: Clay or Play-Doh

1. Identify something your child is feeling worried about. It could be going to school, taking a big test, or sleeping in their own room.

2. Next, have them create a bug out of clay or Play-Doh to represent this worry.

3. Once they have created the bug, have them place it on an uncarpeted floor (one you are comfortable with them smooshing the bug into).

4. Prompt your child to take a deep breath in—then smoosh the worry bug with their feet. Have them notice how it feels to be bigger and stronger than their worry.

5. Let your child make another worry bug or remake the same worry bug as many times as they want. Encourage them to really smoosh the bug!

MASTER MINDFULNESS TIP: Suggest that your child smoosh the bug with their bare feet. Have them notice how the clay or Play-Doh feels beneath their feet as they smoosh it.

CHAPTER 9

Connecting with Nature

Studies show that the more time we spend outside in nature, the better we feel! Spending time outdoors can help both children and adults improve their mood, sleep, and ability to focus. In addition, outdoor play encourages children to engage in big full-body movements, such as climbing a tree or swinging high into the sky. These types of activities can help children build the confidence they need to handle challenges. The activities in this chapter focus on a variety of ways that children can develop mindfulness in the outdoors. Not only do these activities offer guidance on how to weave mindfulness into common outdoor play, they can help you and your child explore and possibly rediscover the power of nature.

Sun Scan

The goal of this activity is to help your child notice how their body feels when they are outdoors in the sun. Use your discretion to determine the length of time you want your child to spend in direct sunlight.

BENEFITS: Mind–Body Connection, Present-Moment Awareness, Calm & Relaxation

1. Choose a place to sit outside where you and your child can both feel the sun comfortably on your body.

2. Have your child close their eyes, if they are comfortable doing so, as you read the following out loud:

   Take a deep breath in. We are going to notice the sun on our bodies. See if you can notice how the sun feels on the different parts of your body.

   a. *Start by noticing the sun shining on just your face. (pause)*

   b. *Now notice the sun shining on your neck. (pause)*

   c. *Notice the sun on your arms. (pause)*

   d. *Notice the sun shining on your belly. (pause)*

   e. *Notice the sun on your legs. (pause)*

   f. *Notice the sun on your feet. (pause)*

   Take a deep breath in and see if you can notice the sun all over you!

3. Ask your child how it felt to notice the sun on their body.

MASTER MINDFULNESS TIP: This game is great to play when you first get outside because it can create a connection to outdoor sensations.

Breathing in Color

The goal of this activity is to help your child bring awareness to their surroundings with a soothing element. The more you practice deep breathing in a playful way, the more likely your child will use this skill in the future.

BENEFITS: **Present-Moment Awareness, Calm & Relaxation**

1. With your child, pick three to five colors that they like.

2. Have them name something each color can give them (for example, red is strength, blue is calm, purple is magic powers, etc.). Allow your child to get as silly and creative with this as they want.

3. Next, explore an outdoor area together, hunting for things of each color.

4. Each time you find an item in nature that is one of your child's chosen colors, have your child take a deep breath in, pretending to breathe in that color's quality from the item. For example, if a red flower is found, your child will breathe in strength. Join your child in taking deep breaths.

5. Repeat until you have collected breaths from all the things you can find in your child's colors!

KEEP PLAYING: **Make this activity silly by pretending every color provides a magic power. Once you and your child have collected all the powers, play together using your magic!**

Freeze Wand

This simple silly game was inspired by the kids who joyfully play together in my neighborhood. The goal of this activity is to mix high intensity movement with stillness, a powerful combination that can help your child build impulse control.

BENEFITS: Focus & Attention, Impulse Control

MATERIALS: Stick

1. Find a stick that is small enough that you and your child can safely run with it.

2. Pick one of you to have the stick—the freeze wand.

3. The goal of the game is to run around together until the person with the freeze wand "freezes" the other person with the wand. The person who becomes frozen has to stay frozen until they take a deep breath.

4. Take turns having the freeze wand—and don't forget to take a deep breath!

KEEP PLAYING: The more the merrier for this game. The more people there are who have to be frozen, the more challenging the game becomes.

Bird Feeder

One way to practice mindfulness is by offering gratitude to others. Expressing gratitude to animals is a great way for children to practice this! This activity walks you and your child through creating a simple bird feeder together while providing an opportunity to practice focused attention.

BENEFITS: Self-Compassion & Confidence, Focus & Attention

MATERIALS: Cheerios or circle-shaped cereal, pipe cleaners

1. Create a bird feeder together by simply stringing Cheerios, or any other circle-shaped cereal, onto a pipe cleaner. String as many or as few pieces of cereal onto the pipe cleaner as you like.

2. As you and your child string the cereal onto the pipe cleaner, send loving and kind thoughts to the birds!

3. Hang the bird feeder outside in a place where your child can easily see it. Encourage your child to check on the feeder and watch the birds come and go!

MASTER MINDFULNESS TIP: Sit outside together and practice focusing your attention on just the birds at the bird feeder. Try to notice the sounds they make as they come and go.

Mud Pie Magic

There is something magical about letting children get messy in the mud. Mud can be a fully immersive sensory experience! This activity is a great way to weave mindfulness into natural play that your child already might enjoy.

BENEFITS: Present-Moment Awareness, Mind–Body Connection

MATERIALS: Mud, sticks, leaves, water, bucket, Frisbee or old pie pan, spoons, clothes that are okay to get dirty

1. With your child, go on a hunt to find different items to decorate a mud pie, for example, flowers, leaves, sticks, stones, and shells.

2. Now gather some mud! Either find some mud already formed in your yard or a nearby park, or mix some dirt with water in a shallow hole in the ground or in a bucket.

3. Next, using hands or a spoon, scoop the mud into the pie pan or Frisbee. Encourage your child to use their hands!

4. Keep them noticing by asking questions like *How does that feel in your hands? Is the mud warm or cold? What do you notice about the smell?*

5. Decorate the mud pie any way your child wishes using the natural materials collected.

KEEP PLAYING: Allow your child to experiment with making the mud different consistencies by pouring different amounts of water into the dirt. Maybe they can even sculpt the mud into a creative shape once they are done making pies.

Barefoot Breathing

An important aspect of mindfulness is learning how to connect to our bodies through our breath. The goal of this activity is for your child to notice a sense of grounding when they place bare feet on the ground and breathe. Something magical happens when we put our bare feet on the ground and pay attention to the sensations.

BENEFITS: Mind–Body Connection, Grounding & Coping Skills, Calm & Relaxation, Present-Moment Awareness

1. Explain to your child that they are going to try to use their feet to breathe. This might sound like:

   Some people believe that when we put our bare feet on the ground and take in a deep breath, we are breathing the air all the way into our feet. This can give us energy, making us feel strong and powerful!

2. Find a place outside where you feel comfortable having your child stand or sit with bare feet.

3. Now have your child place their bare feet on the ground. Instruct them to inhale and exhale slowly.

4. Prompt your child to pay special attention to the way their bare feet feel on the ground as they breathe.

KEEP PLAYING: Have your child try the same activity with their hands. See if they notice a difference in how their body feels when they put their hands on the ground instead of their feet.

Bug's-Eye View

The goal of this activity is for your child to slow down and really notice the world around them. Using their imagination and ability to be present in the moment is a great way for them to practice mindfulness outdoors.

BENEFITS: Present-Moment Awareness, Focus & Attention, Calm & Relaxation

MATERIALS: Blanket, magnifying glass or binoculars (optional)

1. Find a spot on the ground to sit or lie down comfortably on your blanket.

2. Ask your child to use their imagination to pretend they are as tiny as a bug, deep in the grass.

3. Have your child imagine or use the magnifying glass or binoculars (if using) to examine the world around them from the bug's point of view!

4. Encourage your child to stay still and quiet as they pay attention to what they see and hear from this new perspective.

KEEP PLAYING: Using paper and art materials, have your child draw what they saw in the grass.

Mindfulness Hike

Taking your child for a hike may not be a groundbreaking way to spend time together outdoors. But this activity will help you turn this classic outing into a mindfulness adventure for the whole family!

BENEFITS: Present-Moment Awareness, Emotional Expression & Regulation, Focus & Attention, Mind–Body Connection

1. Before starting your hike, explain to your child that you are going to be practicing mindfulness on your adventure.

2. One easy way to practice mindfulness during your outing is by turning on your senses. As you walk along, prompt your child to try to notice things with their senses.

    a. *Try to notice one thing you can **hear**.*

    b. *Try to notice one thing you can **see**.*

    c. *Try to notice one thing you can **smell**.*

    d. *Try to notice one thing you can **feel**.*

KEEP PLAYING: Instead of trying to notice things with all the senses on the hike, pick just one sense (hear, see, smell, feel) and have your child try to notice things with just that sense.

Mindful Walking Path

Many times, when we are out walking, we pay no attention to the actual act of moving our bodies. We are often lost in thought, focused on where we are going or what we are about to do next. Bringing all our attention to the movement is a great way to practice mindfulness. This activity helps your child use their imagination to create a playful path for practicing mindful walking.

BENEFITS: Calm & Relaxation, Creativity & Flexible Thinking, Present-Moment Awareness

MATERIALS: Sidewalk chalk, large rocks, stepping-stones, log rings or pine cones

1. Identify a safe area outside, large enough to make an imaginary path.

2. Next, have your child choose available materials to create a path. This could simply be sidewalk chalk (to use on your driveway) or a collection of pine cones or rocks.

3. Working together, use the materials to design and build a path of any length and shape!

4. Once the path is built, have your child practice walking along the path in slow motion, paying close attention to how their body feels as it moves.

MASTER MINDFULNESS TIP: Many mindfulness masters repeat a mantra as they walk a path. If you have done the Mantra Stone activity (page 102), encourage your child to add their mantra to their walk for added focus.

Natural Gratitude

A lasting impact of mindfulness is that it helps us grow kindness for ourselves and the world around us. This activity is a simple way for your child to bring attention and awareness to the world around them while practicing kindness through gratitude.

BENEFITS: Self-Compassion & Confidence, Present-Moment Awareness

1. Explain to your child how to share kindness in a simple way. This might sound like:

   Today, while we are outside, we will be trying to spread kindness in the world. One way we can do this is by giving attention to something we see, then saying out loud something about that thing we are grateful for.

2. Offer some simple examples of things your child might notice:

   a. *I see my friend Ben's house. I am grateful for how we can play together.*

   b. *I see a flower. I am grateful that it is here for me to smell.*

   c. *I hear a bee buzzing. I am grateful that it helps pollinate our food.*

3. Try to spread kindness this way to as many different things outside as possible.

KEEP PLAYING: Encourage your child to practice sending kindness in this way at bedtime by thinking of different things they noticed throughout the day and what they are grateful for about them.

Resources

Books

Growing Up Mindful: Essential Practices to Help Children, Teens, and Families Find Balance, Calm, and Resilience by Christopher Willard

No-Drama Discipline: The Whole-Brain Way to Calm the Chaos and Nurture Your Child's Developing Mind by Daniel J. Siegel and Tina Payne Bryson

The Whole-Brain Child: 12 Revolutionary Strategies to Nurture your Developing Child's Mind by Daniel J. Siegel and Tina Payne Bryson

Podcasts

Mindful Mama Mentor with Hunter Clarke-Fields

Mindful Parenting in a Messy World with Michelle Gale

The Mindful Parent Podcast with Scott Rogers

Instagram

Big Little Feelings @biglittlefeelings

Busy Toddler @busytoddler

Dr. Becky Kennedy @drbeckyatgoodinside

Playful Families @amycox.co

Websites

Association for Play Therapy (a4pt.org): The Association for Play Therapy is a national organization that focuses on the growth and development of play therapy, play, and credentialed play therapists.

TBRI Skills: Trust-Based Relational Intervention (child.tcu.edu): TBRI is a type of parenting framework designed to help meet the specific challenges faced by parents whose children have experienced trauma.

References

Artigas, Lucina, and Ignacio Jarero. "The Butterfly Hug Method for Bilateral Stimulation." September 2014. emdrfoundation.org/toolkit/butterfly-hug.pdf.

Association for Play Therapy. "Why Play Therapy?" Accessed April 11, 2022. a4pt.org/page/WhyPlayTherapy.

Harper, Jennifer Cohen. *Little Flower Yoga for Kids: A Yoga and Mindfulness Program to Help Your Children Improve Attention and Emotional Balance.* Oakland, CA: New Harbinger, 2013.

Kabat-Zinn, Jon. *Mindfulness for Beginners: Reclaiming the Present Moment— and Your Life.* Boulder, CO: Sounds True, 2012.

Kabat-Zinn, Jon. *Wherever You Go There You Are.* 10th ed. New York: Hachette Books, 2005.

Kestly, Theresa A. *The Interpersonal Neurobiology of Play: Brain-Building Interventions for Emotional Well-Being.* New York: W.W. Norton, 2014.

MBSR Teachers Collaborative of Greater New York. "History of MBSR." Accessed April 11, 2022. mbsrcollaborative.com/history-of-mbsr.

O'Connor, Kevin J., Charles E. Schaefer, and Lisa D. Braverman. *Handbook of Play Therapy.* Hoboken, NJ: John Wiley & Sons, 2016.

Panksepp, Jaak, and Lucy Biven. *The Archaeology of Mind: Neuroevolutionary Origins of Human Emotions.* New York: Norton, 2012.

Plummer, Deborah. *Focusing and Calming Games for Children.* London: Jessica Kingsley Publishers, 2012.

Saltzman, Amy. "Mindfulness: A Guide for Teachers." Accessed April 11, 2022. contemplativemind.org/Mindfulness-A_Teachers_Guide.pdf.

"Why Play Matters." Pittsburgh Toy Lending Library. Accessed June 16, 2022. pghtoys.org/why-play-matters.

Willard, Christopher. *Growing Up Mindful: Essential Practices to Help Children, Teens, and Families Find Balance, Calm, and Resilience.* Boulder, CO: Sounds True, 2016.

Index

Acknowledgments

I want to acknowledge my many mindfulness and yoga teachers. It is through your support and guidance I learned how to share this incredible tool with the world. I am eternally grateful for what these tools have given me.

About the Author

 **Melissa LaVigne** is a licensed clinical social worker, registered play therapist, and registered yoga teacher. She runs a small private practice in Buffalo, New York, where she provides therapy services to children, families, and adults. She specializes in play therapy, mindfulness, and trauma treatment. Melissa is passionate about sharing these tools with the world and, to do so, trains both nationally and internationally on these topics. In addition to her clinical work, Melissa is a faculty member, trainer, and yoga teacher for Yogis in Service and a co-founder of Calm Bodies, Calm Minds, an organization that provides schools with trauma-informed mindfulness tools for the classroom.

Printed in the USA
CPSIA information can be obtained
at www.ICGtesting.com
LVHW060408120124
768705LV00003B/5